The Outhouse Poet

Poet

Reflections of a Writer

PRAISE FOR *The Outhouse Poet*

Frances Kakugawa wrote about growing up in a remote village I came to love, now fossilized under a volcano, in *Echoes of Kapoho*, among my most favorite books of all time. As a fan of Stephen King and Dickens, that's saying a lot. *The Outhouse Poet* is a sequel. Frances really does see into the human heart like few others, making even the hidden-in-plain-sight secret world of retirees who gather at an ordinary shopping mall shine out to us with life's surge. This book brought me laughter, made me misty-eyed a few pages later, then brought laughter again, and warmth. If you haven't encountered Frances before, this introduction is a treat.

Charles Pellegrino, PhD
author, *Ghosts of Hiroshima* and *Her Name, Titanic*

As a young girl, Frances Kakugawa had dreams of becoming a writer and poet as she sat in the Kapoho outhouse. It is where her life journey started, a metaphor for discovering herself when she began to reflect about what her life might become. Now an accomplished and recognized poet and writer, she discovers a new outhouse, a mall where she walks six days a week. Here the mall is a metaphor for discovering valuable lessons about forgiveness, empathy, helpfulness and caring, lessons taught to her by fellow mall walkers, some ephemeral, others long lasting. She writes of poems she has written, of mall walkers she had gotten to know and of memories of life in Kapoho. She is known as the Poet Laureate of the Mall. It is a long way out of the outhouse.

Dean Dorn, PhD
author, *Sociology with a Human Face*

OTHER BOOKS BY FRANCES H. KAKUGAWA

<u>FOR CAREGIVERS</u>

Mosaic Moon: Caregiving Through Poetry

Breaking the Silence: A Caregiver's Voice

I Am Somebody:
Bringing Dignity and Compassion to Alzheimer's Caregiving

<u>CHILDREN'S BOOKS</u>

Wordsworth the Poet

Wordsworth Dances the Waltz

Wordsworth! Stop the Bulldozer!

Wordsworth, It's In Your Pocket!

Wordsworth the Haiku Teacher

<u>MEMOIRS</u>

Teacher, You Look Like a Horse!

Kapoho: Memoir of a Modern Pompeii

Echoes of Kapoho

<u>POETRY</u>

Sand Grains

White Ginger Blossom

Golden Spike

The Path of Butterflies

Dangerous Woman

<u>ANTHOLOGIES</u>

The Kindergarten Dropout of Kapoho

Can I Have Your Pearl Bracelet?

The Outhouse Poet
Reflections of a Writer

Frances H. Kakugawa

WATERMARK
PUBLISHING

ISBN: 978-1-958701-33-1

Library of Congress Control Number: 2025916005

Design and production by Dawn Sakamoto Paiva
Author's photo by Tammy Antonio
Front cover photo: Adobe Stock / World Travel Photos

Watermark Publishing
1088 Bishop Street, LL3
Honolulu, Hawai'i 96813
Telephone (toll-free): 1-866-900-BOOK
Website: www.bookshawaii.net

Printed in the United States of America

This is dedicated with love and gratitude to you who are holding this book in your hands and to all the descendants of the Kapoho outhouse.

FRANCES H. KAKUGAWA

THE OUTHOUSE POET

Table of Contents

FOREWORD

When author Frances Kakugawa invites you to meet her at the outhouse, you should go because you know you're in for a treat. This book and the delightful stories contained herein, drawn from her everyday experiences at the shopping mall and other places, attest to the idea that wisdom can be found all around us, sometimes even in those whom we may least expect to have a life lesson or two to share. And yet these simple exchanges with our fellow human beings often leave us with important, if not profound, insights if we listen not only with our ears but also with open hearts and minds. Frances demonstrates that genuine communication—not only with people who look and think like she does, but with a wide variety of people—can lead to enduring social connections and the kind of positive energy that comes from the convergence of mutual respect, friendly humor and sincere interest in the welfare of others. Her stories of encounters with fellow mall walkers, whom she affectionately refers to as "mall rats," proves the point that a little kindness can go a long way.

This is Frances's nineteenth book, quite an exceptional achievement for this award-winning writer who was born and raised in the rural village of Kapoho on the Big Island of Hawai'i. In an outhouse in a poor but close-knit working-class community, Frances found her quiet place for reading, thinking, and dreaming. Her childhood home and the entire village were destroyed by lava flows from a Kīlauea volcanic eruption when she was in college, and this tale of destruction and resilience became the subject of one of her books later in life. In a sense, the act of writing about the vicissitudes of life with all its tragedy, drama and comedy has come to characterize her books of poetry and prose. She takes the stuff of real life and repurposes it into words that live on in other forms. She has learned that words have a certain power all their own, and is happy to share that power through writing classes and workshops to help others find their literary voices as well.

The Outhouse Poet features stories about kindness and generosity, but true to life, there are also stories about rudeness, racism and disrespect, all things the author herself has experienced firsthand at points in her long life. These negative life experiences have not held her back. They seem to have made her stronger, and whatever anger she felt she has used to fuel her passion for writing. Sometimes negative encounters are inevitable, but we can choose how to use them. We can choose to perpetuate and intensify the negativity by being negative ourselves, or we can choose to try and understand it, defuse it as best we can and then keep moving forward in life with confidence and optimism.

This book draws from the past—Frances's fans will recognize some of her references to topics from previous works—but it is also quite attuned to current events, occasionally infusing social commentary in a pointed but not preachy manner. Her popular children's book character Wordsworth the Poet Mouse and his friends make an appearance, commenting through dialogue on the unfortunate practice of book banning. Because books have been so integral to Frances's personal and professional lives, she holds a special place in her heart for freedom of speech and creative expression.

Although Frances is now ensconced in a suburban Sacramento, California, neighborhood and enjoying the comforts that come with indoor plumbing and electricity, it is clear from her writing that she has never really left Kapoho completely behind. She has carried within her the values of this tiny village that outsiders may have regarded as culturally and economically deprived, but insiders knew was prosperous in so many other ways. Kapoho taught her to see the world through a lens of kindness, community, and gratitude. Frances Kakugawa would not be who she is today without starting her life journey in Kapoho—and thank goodness for that.

On a personal note, discovering this book has been like finding an oasis in the midst of a barren desert. Reading and re-reading these stories has been refreshingly therapeutic at a time in history when hatred, conflict and anger seem to be the unsavory flavors of the day. Frances has lived through wars, poverty and social injustice over her almost nine decades on this earth, and yet her words in writing and in speech exude so much love and compassion for her fellow travelers in life. She embodies the Japanese concept of *omoiyari*—thinking of others first—a value system learned from growing up in a loving family within a community of people who care about each other's well-being. The physical Kapoho may be long gone thanks to the mysterious workings of Madame Pele, the volcano goddess, but its spirit lives on in its former residents.

At a time when calamity and suffering seem to be happening every day somewhere in the world, this book's stories offer rays of hope and joy. They celebrate the power of human relationships—not necessarily the kind between a husband and wife or between two lifelong friends, but the relationships with our neighbors and those we meet at the mall or wherever our community gathering places happen to be. The world around us is a social laboratory. There are opportunities to learn from every human being we encounter if we choose to communicate meaningfully. This is a message that is more important now than ever before; indeed, it is a message that could save the world.

As for meeting Frances Kakugawa at the "outhouse," count me in! I would sit at this woman's feet anytime, anywhere, to listen to her stories and learn, smile and feel good about being alive. Thank you, dear Frances, for continuing to use your gifts to make the world a better place. You remind us that we can all make a positive difference in the world wherever we happen to be: at the mall, in the workplace or even on a plane sitting next to a taciturn stranger who you suspect might have been raised by wolves. So let's put down the smartphones and start making connections of another kind: one soul to another, beginning in our own backyard.

Kevin Y. Kawamoto, MSW, PhD
Gerontological Social Work Educator

Introduction

It began in the Kapoho outhouse. The outhouse was both my hideaway from household chores and my dream house, where fantasies of becoming a writer, a Hollywood actress and a literary celebrity were generated. Yelling "I stay in da toilet!" as loud as I could was my passport to this freedom. I had perfected my yell as a means to be left alone when called to cook the rice or to start the fire under the *furo*. (My father worked as a cane cutter in the sugar plantation fields, and the bath water in the wooden tub had to be heated and ready for his return each day.)

The outhouse was where I leafed through the Sears catalog, our Charmin; the pictures in it fed my fantasies of life beyond Kapoho, a life of evening gowns, tuxedoed men and sophisticated conversation in elegant New York interiors. It was also my library, where I read borrowed magazines featuring Hollywood stars or whatever I could find in the bookmobile.

Our front porch was my second choice for solitude, and it was here that I read banned books. But the porch didn't give me the privacy I craved, since it also served as Kapoho's unofficial Tourist Information Center. Our house was near the village train station, so tourists often stopped to ask for directions to Warm Springs, a natural fresh-water pond where the movie *Bird of Paradise* was filmed with Debra Paget, Louis Jourdan and Jeff Chandler. Warm Springs would be covered by lava some years later.

Although my Kapoho outhouse is also under megatons of lava now thanks to Kīlauea's volcanic eruptions, I recently discovered a place just as capable of inspiring my creativity. My new place has no reeking outhouse odors, no pesky flies, no cockroaches crawling across my butt and no warm dampness rising from below. And no one calling me to cook the rice.

My new outhouse, which I found at the height of the COVID-19 pandemic, is our neighborhood shopping mall, located just behind our back fence. Each day I walk inside the large mall for over an hour before the shops open, and what a rich source of inspiration these walks have been! This volume is a collection of stories and poems rooted in my mall walks. Some names have been changed to protect privacy, though many of my mall-walking friends granted me permission to use their given names. And an outhouse by any other name is still an outhouse.

Outhouse

A house unpainted:
corrugated roof, four walls.
Floor, six feet by two and a half.
Redwood seat with two round holes
sized to accommodate adults.
Balanced on old railroad ties
squared over a bottomless pit.
It is here she sits and answers
Nature's Call.

The fear of falling through
turns her knuckles white
as she holds on to the edge
of the wooden seat.
A generic outhouse,
unlike a neighbor's
where an additional hole,
smaller in size,
makes it a seat for three.

A wooden apple box against a wall,
filled with square red apple wrappers,
greets her with faint apple scent,
but only for a moment.

At arm's reach, torn sheets of
the *Hilo Tribune Herald*
hang on a nail.
On the floor, Sears and Montgomery Ward,
pages of dreams, her Charmin.

Right out the door, a peach tree
reaches toward the sky.
During blossom season,
the scent of peach petals
can't overcome the stench.
No flies, no gnats, only cockroaches
scurrying across her butt.
Dampness and heat rise from below.

Every outhouse has its own smell.
She gags and holds her nose
without breathing
in other people's outhouses,
but seldom uses them,
preferring to race home
when the need arises.

This is her place of refuge,
a place where her need
for undisturbed solitude
is respected, a place
where she sits and reads
books, comics, *True Confessions*
cover to cover,
and *Life in These United States*.

From here she shouts,
"I stay in da toilet!"when called to do the dishes
or start the rice.
It is a shout she has perfected
after years of practice, heard
in all the neighboring houses,
for what parent would dare call again
to ask her to do chores
when Nature's Call came first?
It is her House of Literacy.

THE MALL RATS

She approached me at the mall with "Hello, my name is Judy. A good way to remember me is to think of me as Judy Garland. I attach famous names to people to help me remember them. See those two ladies? Their names are Diana and Elizabeth, and I think of them as the Princess and the Queen. That man, Hugh, remember him as Hugh Hefner.""So, Judy," I asked. "Who am I?"

She couldn't think of any famous person called Frances.

"Well," I offered, "I guess I'm Frances the Talking Mule."

A few days later I heard "Frances!" I turned and saw Judy.

"I'm Judy, Judy Garland."

"So, Judy," I asked, "Did you think of a mule before you called me?"

"Oh no," she said, "I know who you are."

One morning, I was walking with fellow walker Hugh. Judy stopped us to say, "I'm having foot surgery next week, so I won't be here for at least six weeks, just in case you wonder where I am."

"Do you have someone to care for you?" I asked.

"Yes," she assured me, "I have." I wished her well and told Hugh I was going to offer Judy his help if she didn't have anyone. He gave me a glare with laughter in his eyes. One day, some months after telling me of her newly diagnosed cancer, Judy stopped appearing at the mall. This saddened me, especially since she had been so upbeat before her radiation treatment.

To me, Hugh is more a Fix-It Man than a Hefner: He can rebuild a car with all the parts lying on the ground. He knows how to repair and even regenerate an old battery. Hugh had worked at a gym repairing equipment, and due to the mold and bacteria found in gyms he lost almost half of his lung capacity.

In 2009, he was given two weeks to live. "You won't make it to your next appointment," his doctor told him. Exercising his quick wit, Hugh retorted, "Better keep me alive if you want to get paid." He is still here; he either hasn't paid his doctor's bills or was met with a medical miracle.

His passion is the ten acres he owns in the foothills. He spends his time working on his cabin and clearing the land of brush and dead trees. One day while we were walking, a friend called him on his cell and asked him about the woman he had picked up on his walks. I took the phone and told his friend, "Hugh has excellent taste in women but the only reason I allow him to walk with me is to inherit his ten acres."

His father was at Pearl Harbor on December 7 and had to drag bodies out of the water. Hugh has visited Hawai'i often because of his father's ties there. After months of walking together, I asked about his father's attitude toward the Japanese.

"Oh, his best friends were Japanese. My dad hated the internment camps because his friends and their families were being sent there." This told me I could share my *Echoes of Kapoho* book with him so he could learn of how it was for us Japanese Americans. He shared the book with his sister, who sent me little gifts through her brother, in appreciation for the book.

I have befriended four men who sit around the same table at the Food Court, using the Judy Garland system. For their names, I call it the Presidents' Table except for Bob whom I've named Bob the Reader. He is there seven days a week with a book and a bottle of Diet Coke, and he was reading the entire works of Jules Verne when I interrupted him one day. When I asked him about poetry, he said, "I don't really read poetry." That was a challenge I couldn't resist, so I gave him my *Dangerous Woman: Poetry for the Ageless*. After a few weeks he said he had read the book and marked a few poems but didn't know why he had marked them. There are no secrets at the mall, and soon the men around the Presidents'

Table started asking if I had changed Bob's mind about poetry. Not yet.

So we talk books and share little sketches from our lives. An excellent gardener, he has sent me home with tomatoes, zucchini, cucumbers and squash. He also bakes the best brownies ever with his secret recipe.

The three other men at the Presidents' Table all sit in their same designated chairs. There is Ron (Reagan), Tom (Jefferson) and Cal (Coolidge). Tom, who is thin as a whistle, comes to the table with biographies and his cell phone. He had the biography of Jackie Kennedy for over a month and is now reading about the Mamas and the Papas. "I met Mama Cass in Vegas once," I shared. "She was doing a solo show and I was in the second row. Her monologue began with some Asian jokes and she kept looking at me to gauge my reaction. I clapped my hands and laughed, and she nodded at me and later came to shake my hand. I was her non-censor monitor for the evening." Whether that impressed Tom, I couldn't tell, since he seldom speaks or makes eye contact. His passions are baseball, *Star Wars*, building with Legos and games on his iPhone. He dislikes wind and rain because the bicycle is his sole means of transportation. He does glare at me when I mention how I love rain and winter.

For months, I hesitated to sit with the Presidents because the chairs seemed to have invisible "Reserved" signs, but one day I dragged a chair over to join the conversation. Days later, Bob mentioned how I was finally sitting with them, which apparently was all it took to make me one of the guys at the Presidents' Table.

Cal, who had worked in a university bookstore, is the only one who wears a mask as I do. One day he stopped me to ask if I had my COVID vaccination, because they were now available. He keeps me updated on vaccines and such matters as the recent law allowing the elderly to renew driver's licenses without taking a written test. Once when I complimented him on challenging others whose views differ from us, Cal said something wise, "If I have the facts to support me, I will challenge others who seem confused about climate change and certain political positions."

Ron always wears a dress shirt with matching hats, a dapper Rex Harrison.

He explained his reason: He had worked in construction and decided he wanted to dress up after retiring. His wife joins us now and then. Bob prefers T-shirts after years of wearing a suit and tie as a manager in a large department store.

Jane (Powell) works at the Korean takeout counter in the mall's food court. She mothers Bob the Reader and me, like Mama Bear protecting her cubs. Before I go on trips I give her the dates so she won't wonder about my absence. I return with little gifts which give her much delight. She complains about Bob not having a cell phone because how can she check on him when he's absent.

She makes *kimchi* to my liking without sesame oil and seeds and with less hot pepper. For a long time, her oft-repeated advice to me was "Never Get Married," as if I were a young woman. Then one day, she changed her conversation to, "Oh good, good that you walk every day. Good exercise!"

Bob laughed and told me Jane had been trying to guess my age, so he told her I was born before Pearl Harbor was bombed, which he had discovered when he read my *Echoes of Kapoho* book. "Bob!" I elbowed him. "So this is why she now talks to me as if I'm an old old lady. It's you! You blew my cover!"

I have such a sense of loyalty that when I purchase anything somewhere other than Jane's Korean takeout, I sneak past Jane with my purchases. Loyalty often demands covert behavior.

There are two elegant ladies who stop by to say hello. Deni (Thomas) dresses like a woman on her way to a tea party and greets each of us graciously. She knows almost all the mall regulars by name, including cleaning staff, repairmen, security guards and salespeople. Elegant Shelly (Winters), who is always nicely coiffed, listens to our chatter with few comments. She must have more shoes than Imelda Marcos; all her outfits have matching footwear. She's in her nineties, so I must hold the title of second-oldest walker.

One day I walked into a conversation on death and dying at the Presidents' Table. The men were discussing their cemetery plots and postmortem funeral arrangements. Tom complained that they ought to stop talking about death. I suggested we needed to talk about it for the sake of our survivors and make plans so they will know exactly what to do. I mentioned that I have donated my body to UC Davis Medical Center, so should I drop dead, they need to call UC Davis immediately.

"Oh," said Ron, "Maybe we can get some body parts first."

Bob the Reader added, "We'll just donate you to the Korean takeout."

I said, "Yeah, the kalbi will be the best ever. Who do you think you all are, Stephen King?"

This is commonplace talk where Bob and I try to out-insult each other. On Valentine's Day when Anna passed out treats, he greeted me with, "Mine said 'I am cute.' Did yours say 'I am ugly?'" Only friends can talk like this.

Dean (Martin) is a sociology professor emeritus who has taught for more than thirty-five years. We stop to chat daily. He has given me different perspectives on some of my books from his sociological background, adding how he would have used some of my work in his sociology classes. We were born the same year so each morning we greet each other with "We are here!" He often recites lines from my poetry just as I recite lines from Emily Dickinson.

Then there is Anna (Karenina) who taught me how to straighten my posture. She floats effortlessly like a cloud, back straight as a flagpole, head unbowed, looking ahead. I stopped her to admire her posture, since I'm beginning to slouch the way my mother did. "The secret," she advised, "is a backpack. Use a backpack and it will improve your posture." I now walk with a backpack and each time I see her, I straighten my spine.

In addition to about a dozen workers and walkers, there are three couples with whom I exchange greetings and stop to chat. We inform each other of any upcoming absences. We joke and laugh and exchange thumbs up as we pass each other. I stopped them one day to say, "I read in the *New York Times* this morning that belly laughs keep us healthy and alive. You're keeping me alive."

Frank (Sinatra) Poppy and his wife, Lordes, greet me affectionately each morning. Frank enters my thoughts whenever I stray into hypochondria because he lives with his serious illness with such acceptance and hope. "I'm ready for the Lord any day," he says. I call him my inspiration to live each day as though it were my last.

Frank, a truck driver, has driven across the country without a single driving citation.

He and Lordes dated at age sixteen, got married at eighteen, and their lifelong devotion is touching, still holding hands like teenagers. He keeps me on my toes with his fast retorts, resulting in belly laughs.

Security guard Mike (Moore) and his wife, Virgie, world travelers, have become friends outside of the mall. When I hear my name from the second floor, I know it's Mike greeting me.

John (Wayne) and Michaela can be recognized from afar because they're holding hands. When they're absent, they're traveling to some exotic places. Mikaela invited me to speak to a women's organization that raises college scholarship funds for needy students in the Sacramento area. The group met in Michaela's home and I talked about how I fulfilled the dream I had at age six of becoming a writer. I spoke of the college scholarship I was granted, which opened the door to higher education for me, and of the donor who came to our house every summer to ask me one question only: "Do you have a boyfriend? No? Good, you finish college first." Years later, when he read about my first published book of poetry, he wrote, "When I told you not to have a boyfriend, I didn't mean forever. Nothing would please me more than to receive a wedding invitation from you." I would later donate funds for a similar scholarship at my alma mater. It was heartwarming to know what that donor had done for me was still being done by Michaela and her group of ladies.

John gives me belly laughs with his jokes and puns that are a step above Dad jokes.

What do snowmen love to eat for breakfast? Frosted Flakes!

If you take a piece of fancy writing paper and fold it into a paper airplane, and then throw it as hard as you can, it's still stationery!

One month I gave a lecture for the Alzheimer's Association. Bob the Reader had passed out the flyer without my knowledge and I was moved to see him and Mike and his wife in attendance. Both said they later shared some of the information from my lecture with friends who were caregivers.

Holidays are special and my pockets get filled with treats during Christmas, Valentine's Day and on Easter by fellow walkers. Today I received birthday cards and gifts from some of my friends at the mall. How they knew of my birthday remains a mystery, but I suspect an active coconut wireless is to blame. I thanked Anna with the following poem:

Thank You

It's not a loaf of bread
It's not a jug of wine.
No, Omar Khayyam,
It's a warm cinnamon roll
With a mug of hot coffee
On the wooden porch
Counting birds on telephone wires.
That's Paradise enow.

Except for Dean and Cal, I don't know much of the politics or home life of the others, and only a few of us have exchanged phone numbers. I am careful about sharing my poems and personal opinions with other walkers, out of respect for differing political and religious beliefs. We are simply mall rats who care for each other; a community of walkers, retirees, security guards, sales and cleaning and repair people who greet each other by name. Cal has turned out to be the caretaker at the Presidents' Table who will call those who are absent for a few days.

Like ants carrying crumbs to their nest, stopping to rub antennae with other ants they meet along the way, we wave, we say good morning, chat and wish each other the best each day. We are sure to inform others when we're unable to be at the mall. Once I had failed to inform the walkers of my doctor's appointment, so the question that day was: Where's Frances? Hugh spread the rumor that I had run off with one of the walkers.

This microcosm of community life reflects a large reality. Some of us begin to use canes, walkers and wheelchairs. A few are no longer seen due to illnesses or deaths. So we walk the mall, knowing life is what it is: temporary and ever-changing. But we are thankful for each day we are here.

The Gardener and Hosea

I have watched enough *NCIS* to know that a camera can pinpoint to the minute the exact time a crime has been committed and a blurred face can be recognized through advanced technology. I should have remembered this as I worked toward becoming a thief.

Often, the security guards and I are the only ones in the mall early in the morning. Beautiful potted plants line the mall on both floors spaced every twenty steps or so. Palms and other trees reach for the roof toward the sun's rays. Gazing between their leafy branches on the second floor, I imagine myself a robin with a delightful bird's-eye view of ground level. Special flowers and plants appear at each holiday: red poinsettias for Christmas, red anthuriums for Valentine's Day, orange and bronze mums for Halloween and Thanksgiving.

One of those potted plants sells for $27 or more at nurseries and supermarkets, yet they grow wild in Hawaiian yards. Why couldn't I just snip off a cutting and start my plant? Who would miss a five-inch cutting? In one out-of-the-way corner of the mall are tucked a couple of plants I could easily trim, hiding the cuttings in my pocket. Each time I passed those potted plants, I stopped and thought, "It wouldn't hurt anyone, just a break off a little stem." Then one day a security guard, in an attempt to assure me that the mall is safe, said, "There are more than 150 cameras in the ceilings."

I took a huge gulp. I could have been arrested for stealing! But I considered going ahead with the theft anyway: will they handcuff an Asian woman, masked, who steals a few inches from a plant?

Two days ago, I saw the gardener working with the plants. I asked to see his trash bag for any cuttings. I told him how pricey those potted plants were, and he asked which plants did I like? Without a word he took out two potted plants, put them in a plastic bag and said, "Walk with me and show me what other plants you want." I told him those two pots were enough. "These are heavy. Let me carry these to your car." He refused the cash I offered him for his lunch. I saw him again today and he asked, "Where is your car? I have a heavy plant for you."

"I can carry that," I said, after thanking him.

"If security stops you, tell them Jose gave it to you," he cautioned, as I took the palm tree to my car. I was not aware we were being observed by Hugh, and soon after he brought me potted plants. I treasure the "Mother of Thousands" kalanchoe he gave me one day.

The kind gardener not only saved me from prison, but he brought unexpected kindness into my life on a mundane Monday morning.

***

Then there is Hosea who taught me that we can also be bearers of joy into a world as ordinary as a mall.

He enters the mall the same time I do, at nine o'clock when doors are opened and sits at a table for an hour. At ten o'clock, he leaves his belongings and goes to the second floor, where he makes his rounds in the food court to sample foods. He always wears the same long-sleeved flannel shirt and looks like any other walker. He has a small carry-on bag and plastic bags bulging with his belongings.

Each day we nodded at each other with "good morning" until one day I gave him a ziplock bag with two masks and a twenty-dollar bill. His face lit up with a smile that became mine when he thanked me. The next day he stopped me to say how I had made his day. We introduced ourselves and he was now Hosea.

Someday I hope to ask Hosea for his story. A fellow walker warned me with his own story: When you see guys coming to the mall with a suitcase and plastic bags of stuff, they probably just came out of prison. They're given about $300 with no place to go.

Last week I took my old large suitcase with wheels and asked Hosea if he could use it. He stood up, turned round and round with both hands up and began to yell, "Whoo! Whoo! Yeah! Yeah!" I left him while he was still dancing around the luggage. I'm not sure who was happier.

The next day, instead of leaving his belongings on the first floor behind as he escalated to the second floor, I saw him with the suitcase, sitting at the food court. He pointed at it and said, "That's a Mercedes."

This week I finally stopped to ask Hosea, "Hosea, will you tell me your story? How did you get here?" He told me as much as he could. He is alone in Sacramento, his family is in South Carolina and he's waiting to return to them. But first, he's waiting for a settlement so he can afford travel fare. "There is so much red tape, you won't believe it," he explained. "The worst part is waiting on all these lies they tell me. I can't go anywhere without this call."

"Who owes you a settlement, Hosea?"

"The Government," he said. "I'll know this Friday if the settlement is approved."

I put my hands together and wished him well.

On Wednesday, I gave him another $20 bill, saying, "This is good luck money for Friday, Hosea." He was too emotional to thank me. I asked, "How will you learn of the decision on Friday?"

"By telephone," he said. I put my hand on his shoulder, not knowing that would be our final good-bye.

On Thursday, for the first time in months, he was not there. I hope his phone call came through earlier than expected although I had wanted to say good-bye to him with a few pairs of socks or even a new shirt.

Today is Friday and he isn't here again. The table where he sat every day appears forlorn. I thought of asking one of the security guards about Hosea; they seem to know everything about everyone in the mall, from which take-out restaurant is behind in their rent to who's going on a trip soon. I decided my story had a better ending: Hosea on his way home with his Mercedes luggage.

Robots vs. Humans

The young adults at the mall seem deaf, blind and mute to the elders who walk among them. I have yet to have a conversation or develop a friendship with the young adults who walk the mall before reporting to work, except for Maria (Callas). Maria, a young diamond consultant in a jewelry shop approached me one day to ask, "Are you the poet? I love to read poetry." She now greets me with a hug, calling me "Hon" affectionately. She brings me fresh vegetables from her garden and keeps my poetry books at her bedside.

We are invisible to the young workers glued to their cell phones. One day I greeted a young woman with, "Good morning." She turned her head, looked at me and said, "Oh, okay," and returned to her cell phone. Another morning I greeted a young woman. She looked at me, paused and said, "Yup," and swiftly returned to the device in her hand.

This morning I saw a young woman standing in front of a shop, waiting for the doors to open at 10:00 a.m. She had her arms around a young man, snuggling against him. When she reached up and kissed him, he continued staring at his cell phone without acknowledging her kiss or glancing at her.

I often encounter these adults in airplanes, sitting next to them as they say not a word from departure to arrival, attached to their technology for the entire flight. Are we letting wolves raise our children? They remind me of a young man who sat next to me on a flight to Hawai'i.

Raised by Wolves

A young man buckles himself next to me,
Connected to wires and earbuds.
He grunts to my Hello without meeting my eyes.
Soon we are flying over the Pacific
Nary a word exchanged.

An hour into flight, breakfast trays appear.
He leans over his mushroom cheese crepes,
Stabs his fork into one, lifts the crepe to his mouth,
Takes a bite and drops the rest of the crepe to his
    plate.
He was raised by wolves, this much I know.

He picks up a wedge of cantaloupe with his fingers
Takes a bite, moves his face over his tray and drops
The remaining portion from mouth to plate.
Utensils, ignored like the napkin on his tray.
My teacher mode kicks in.

Learn by observing, child raised by wolves.
Learn by observing.

Miss Manners and Emily Post at your service
I use each piece of silverware and my napkin, too.
Attempt again for conversation over breakfast.

"Let me guess," I begin.
No, no, I didn't ask, "Were you raised by wolves?"
Miss Manners was still around.
"You're a college student returning home for
    summer break."
He flashes his first smile. He finished his junior year
    in college,
Flying home with hopes of finding a summer job.

I drink my cup of decaf coffee, wish him well.
I was wrong, not raised by wolves, perhaps
By Burger King, finger foods and his Smart Phone.

On the other hand, I have had some rich encounters with people unhampered by electronic devices.

A passenger once sat next to me, opened a thick technical book and after a brief hello, began reading. An hour into flight, I leaned over and asked, "Do you ever read the comics?" He burst out laughing and explained he was reading his newly published book on teaching social studies and was on his way to a job interview at the East-West Center at the University of Hawai'i. Fast forward: I used his book in my teacher training workshops and helped him find a school for his two children.

On another flight, I watched my neighbor work on the in-flight crossword puzzle. Eventually he filled in all the blanks, and I praised his knowledge. Before we disembarked, he came to tell me he had cheated, filling all the spaces with random letters to impress me. Fun!

Again in a plane, a young boy doing a crossword puzzle three aisles away leaned over to ask me, "What was the old name of Tokyo?"

"Edo," I replied, and he gave me a thumbs up. He waited for me as we disembarked and thanked me for my help.

Once while I was reading in an airport lounge, a man told me he knew the father of the book's author, so I learned about the writer's personal life. Had I been engrossed in an e-book, he could not have seen what I was reading, and we would have had no interaction.

Recently I gave a talk to over three hundred students on the subject of poetry. I used my series of children's books about Wordsworth, the little mouse poet who resolves human problems with poetry, as the basis for my talk. One teacher walked into the auditorium with his students, sat down, and took out his cell phone. He didn't listen to my presentation or to the questions his students asked me. Finally, I referred to the book where Wordsworth addresses addiction to technology, and I saw the teacher slowly put his cell phone away. What he missed earlier included a conversation I had with one of his students:

Student: Are you Japanese?

Me: Yes.

Student hugged me and said in Japanese: Thank you so very much. I have not felt such joy. Being different like Wordsworth the Poet can be special.

As they were leaving, the student stepped out of line, approached me, bowed very deeply and said in Japanese, "Thank you very much." The students stared at her, and I was so moved that Wordsworth and our discussion had given her the courage to step up to acknowledge being different. She hoped her fellow classmates would accept her, but if they did not, it didn't matter. The teacher had missed all of this too; he was waiting at the head of the line, once again staring at his cell phone.

Back at the mall, a young woman stunned Bob the Reader when she asked, "What time is noon?" It was a very serious question. She made me wish I were back in the classroom teaching first graders how to tell time, using a large clock with visible hands and numbers and introducing noon and midnight.

One day at a coffee shop I frequented, the cash register was broken and the cashier didn't know how to figure sales tax. I asked for a sheet of paper and wrote down the formula for sales tax calculation. That sheet was on the wall for the rest of the year. The proprietor must have thought using it made more economic sense than purchasing a new cash register. A regular customer and World War II veteran heard my lesson to the cashier and mumbled, "Damn these kids, they only fool around in school and don't learn." I responded, "Maybe it's the damn teacher who didn't teach them." Assigning blame solves no problems, it only relieves us of responsibility for solutions.

To Children of the 21st Century

How do you keep your fingers so free of dirt?
How do you come in from play without
Mud on your feet, your clothes, your cheeks?
How do you not even sweat?

Do you know how rain feels
Soaking your shirt to your skin?
The smell of sea salt in your hair
After a dip in the sea?

Have you watched a little seed
Pushing its first shoot
Out of soil you patted down
A few weeks ago?

Can you see a cardinal, a mynah,
A crow, with your eyes closed, listening
To their signature songs serenaded
In your own back yard?

Have you ever used the eraser
At the end of a pencil,
Writing a poem, a song, a story.
A thank you note?

Do you know the feel of crisp
New pages of a book, as they unfold,
Moving plots, faster than your impatient
Fingers can follow your eyes

Don't you miss sharing eye contact
With the person sitting beside you?
How do you spend time with your friend
Without conversation?

Oh Children of the 21st Century,
Why is there silence in a room filled
With family on this holiday?
How did you become so mute?

Do you know the feel of your grandpa's grip
Warm and strong in your hand?
The story behind that long scar that runs
The length of his arm?

Do you carry memories
Of your grandma's smiles
Each time you said,
Hi Grandma. Can I help you?

Do you ever count clouds, lying
On soft green grass, laughing
Over silly stuff shared with a friend?
Do you ever cry over a child starving

In Africa or in your neighborhood?
Feel upset over trees being cut
For freeways and shopping malls,
Subdivisions and sports arenas?

Do you know what it means to be kind
Compassionate, giving.
To someone whose mirror
Doesn't reflect your face?

Oh, Children of the 21st Century,
Forgive us, for what we have done.

The Mall Poet Laureate

Most poets fantasize about winning a Pulitzer or Nobel Prize. But when you're from the Kapoho outhouse, being crowned Mall Poet is more than one can ask or imagine.

One morning at the end of my walk, without fanfare, Bob the Reader presented me with the Mall Poet Laureate medal. The gold medal hung from a rich satin ribbon, with "Poet Laureate" and my name misspelled on the back. Receiving this from Bob, who doesn't like poetry, was overwhelming. Walking out with the medal draped over my sweatshirt, it brought back memories of my trip to Sweden over sixty years ago.

A large group of travelers from the University of Hawai'i was visiting the building in Stockholm where the Nobel Prizes are awarded each year. A representative from the building stood before us, pointed at me and said, "You will receive the Nobel Prize for Literature today. I will take all of you through the process of how this award is presented." He gave me his arm and we walked up the steps to the entrance, an entourage of tourists close behind us. "Note the low steps," he cautioned. "They are low so the ladies won't step on the gowns." We entered an austere room, and I was presented the imaginary award.

Young and hopeful of someday becoming a writer, I couldn't help thinking this role play might be an omen of things to come. At the mall decades later, as Bob draped the medal over my head, giving me a token of friendship more valuable than the $135,000 Nobel Prize, I was back in Sweden. My youthful dream had been fulfilled in a way I could never have anticipated.

On December 21, 2023, I was officially crowned the Mall Poet Laureate in a low-key group ceremony around the Presidents' Table. A paper plate featuring Bob's home-baked Christmas cookies served as a centerpiece. Each person took the medal to admire it, and I knew I was among the dearest of friends, friends who knew nothing about me except that I wrote poetry.

Since the honors, mall walkers have stopped me to say:

"I Googled you and read your Kapoho book."

"I like your poetry."

Jane from the Korean takeout counter has an adult son who likes to write, and she brought him in to meet me. Mike, the security guard, informed me that new hires are told about the Mall Poet and her morning walks.

The Mall Poet designation even comes with special privileges. When journalist Holly McDede and a photographer from UC Berkeley were doing a story on my work with poetry for caregivers, mall security refused them entrance because of a "no photographers" policy. We asked the guard to call management, who granted immediate admission on mention of the Mall Poet's name.

When Maria (Callas), the diamond consultant from a jewelry shop, stopped to ask me, "Are you the poet?" it took me a moment to respond. Before becoming Mall Poet Laureate, I never answered that question with a "Yes." "Yes" would mean I was in the company of beloved poets like Sandburg, Frost, Dickinson, Shakespeare, Morrison, Wordsworth, Plath—and I was sure I didn't belong there. My response was always a hesitant, "Well, I do write poetry." To Maria that day, I said, "Yes."

The growing respect I see for poetry is as precious to me as the friendships developed at the mall. Now if I should see Bob the Reader and other members of the Presidents' Table all reading a poetry book, I will have earned the title of Mall Poet Laureate.

Mall Poet at Work

She seemed different, walking with sadness on her face. We have never spoken, though we greet each other with a tiny wave at a distance, our palms spread like fans. Her sadness was a blue aura that extended into the mall. The best information center is the security guard, so I inquired and was told her usual walking partner, her husband, had dementia and she had moved him into a nursing home. I knew that sadness as I, too, had placed my mother with Alzheimer's in a nursing facility in Hawai'i. Mall Poet reporting for duty. I gave her a copy of my book *I Am Somebody: Bringing Dignity and Compassion to Alzheimer's Caregiving.*

We have not exchanged names, so I added a note: *I wrote this before placing my mother in a nursing facility. Writing poetry often gives us a new reality or truth. Go to pages 210-212 for this poem.*

Dear Caregiver

I am a burden
Whether the sun greets you
From ocean blue skies,
On a picture perfect morn.
I am a burden,

Whether you gulp in this near perfection
To make it yours,
Forgetting for a moment
I am here.

I am a burden,
Whether dark clouds
Hover over the city,
Forecasting rain
On a Sunday afternoon,
Filling you with an ache
That has no name at all,
I am a burden.

Whether the moon is full or new
In this house that is silenced
By fragmented sleep,
I am a burden.

We live with two thieves, you and I,
And I have become the greater thief
Chiseling away at you
Inch by inch, hour by hour,
Turning you into a kaleidoscope.

Alzheimer's, my nemesis,
No one can yet destroy
But the thief that I have become
Can be expunged.
Free yourself from this thief
With the bond that once existed.

Squeezing out urine from carpets and bedding,
Scrubbing bathroom tiles at 3 a.m.,
Staying up nights, answering his constant calls,
Using your diminishing strength to transport
A thief almost twice your size
Is an act of pure sacrifice,
An act that shatters me like fallen crystal.
It is no longer an act of love,
But one of burden.

We were not joined by blood or vows
For this kind of loving.
The thief has left me with needs
Anyone not bearing your name can meet.
The love that I needed, you have given
Before there was a thief.

We have bade farewell, you and I,
When there was a me.
Let me go before you begin
To crawl in debris of self-destruction.
Set me free in a nursing home
Where the thief I have become
Can no longer be.

To your courage, your love and loyalty
To want to rise above the burden of care,
I press my palms together to you.
But listen to my unspoken words,
It's time to be free.

Free from guilt, sorrow,
Physical and spiritual destruction.
Let us both know peace.
Return us to who we were.

There are no secrets at the mall. I am now a caregiver's poet. A woman shared how difficult it was to visit her mother at a nursing facility because of her diminishing verbal skills. I gave her a copy of this unpublished poem advising her to be mindful of not asking too many questions, as they become a burden to someone with dementia. Sometimes it's nice to make friends with silence.

Tick Tock, Tick Tock

Oh, oh, the test giver is here.
Didn't I take my SAT in high school?
Didn't I pass the Bar years ago?
Why is she here?

Here comes the test:
What did you have for breakfast, Mom?
How was dinner last night? What did you have?
Tick Tock. Tick Tock.
Oh no, what did I eat this morning?
I need more than a second.
Wait, wait. It'll come.
Tick Tock. Tick Tock.

Worse than the Bar, worse than college finals,
My mind aches, my heart beats.
My words have gone hide and go seek.
Tick Tock. Tick Tock.
I can't remember.
Did John visit you yesterday?
Tick Tock. Tick Tock.
Did he? I can't remember.

I'll close my eyes and maybe she'll leave.
Tick Tock. Tick Tock.
Ah good, she's gone.
Who cares about what I ate.
I'd rather take the SAT or the Bar.
Than to be put on trial
On things I don't know.

Oh, oh, another visitor.
Oh, I like him.
He tells me stories.
Yesterday I laughed
When he told me how he spilled his coffee
All over his shirt before his meeting.
I like the songs he sings—
Sometimes I sing along.
Today he's sitting with his leg on my bed,
Reading. That's nice.
I like how he smiles at me before
He turns each page with his fingers.
I like this silence.

My heart is calm, there's no test,
It's like being at the beach,
Watching the waves come in.
Ah...this is nice.
No tick tock, tick tock
Not even for a second.

The Mall Poet earned part of her medal by turning two walkers into poets, which isn't a high average. One morning, Ron (Reagan) presented me a piece of his handwritten prose:

I once was young; now I am old. While young, I saw little, now I see more. When I was young

I lived for today, now I live today. In my youth, I saw little, now in my old age I see much. While young I lived for the day, now old, I live for tomorrow, for tomorrow will come to all who live today.

When I returned his writing in poetic form the following morning and told him, "You are a poet!" his smile made my day. He read it, folded it and put it into his jacket pocket.

I once was young—
Now I am old.
While young I saw little,
Now I see more.
When I was young,
I lived for today.

Now I live today.
In my youth I saw little,
Now in my old age,
I see much more.
While young,
I lived for the day,
Now old, I live for tomorrow,
For tomorrow will come to all
Who live today.

1-1-2024

Dean handed me the following poem one day:

Mall Walkers

The birds go on and on
With their birdy life.

The dogs go on and on
With their doggy life.

While we go on and on
With our antiseptic mall life

I'm waiting to get a poem from Bob the Reader who claims poetry is not his thing.

Last week I gave him a collection of poems written during my ten-day vacation on Whidbey Island in Washington. Included is a poem about a yellow ribbon

I had a friend tie around a street sign so we could find our way back to our rented cottage since we were often missing the street.

Yellow Ribbon

The bow was hung around a road sign post,
a yellow ribbon tied in a left-handed way,
to find our way home and not get confused
by hard-to-read signs at the end of the day,
by forests and farms that left us few clues,
up hills, over bridges, down hills, round bends
to meet once again, as all of us knew,
spectacular sunsets, the fading of day
in turns and U-turns, and a lot of dead-ends.

Barely a footprint remained when we left,
a few trinkets and stories were all that we took,
with the silence of trees, songs of the sea,
spectacular sunsets, farewells to our hosts
we carried back home as fond memories.

We three women then said good-bye
to the Island of Whidbey and the roadside post
where passing travelers still get no answer
from our yellow ribbon's silence to the question,
"Why?"

The next day, there was a yellow ribbon tied to a chair at the entrance of the food court, followed by more yellow ribbons leading me to the table where Bob sat.

I was moved to tears, knowing what Bob had done and why.

"When I read your 'Yellow Ribbon' poem, I knew exactly what I was going to do. I asked Security for permission, and he gave me the number for the mall administrator. I explained that I wanted to tie some ribbons, to help the Mall Poet find her way. She said I could leave the ribbons out for only an hour, since she didn't want to set a precedent for others to add unsolicited ads or other décor to the mall."

Bob has read my poem so I'm not a complete failure, but the Mall Poet still has a lot of work ahead of her.

When Bob brought his best brownies to the Presidents' Table one morning, I wrote and offered him this poem:

Joy

Sometimes the true feeling of joy
Comes not from a grandiose set of events
But from a simple cup of coffee—
Morsels from Bob's secret recipe brownies
On a quiet Friday morning
With no one for company
But one's own thoughts.
Ah...such simple joy...
Such simple joy.

The poem was printed on a sheet of paper that was a bit stiffer than Charmin.

Black Is Not for Old People

I made a woman cry yesterday. During my walk, an older woman stood before the newly opened H&M dress shop and said, "I feel so depressed. All the clothes are black and grey. I guess winter is coming. It's a depressing time."

I was glad I was wearing a bright blouse over my tank top when I told her, "My mother always told me that when we become old, we need to wear bright colors. Black and dull colors are good when you're young. So when she was in her eighties, I dressed her in lavender, light blue and pink."

A tear began to roll down the woman's face. She didn't wipe it away and let it flow down to her chin. She nodded and said, "Your mother was a very wise woman." The next day she wore a flowered pink blouse with a hint of matching lipstick.

I thought of my mother's last words to her Buddhist minister before she died. She came out of her dementia state and was able to say in Japanese: *Watashi wo wasure sasanaide.* Do not let me be forgotten. She was remembered today in the best possible way: Her words offered comfort to a special woman.

The encounter today reminded me of the day I dressed my mother in brown for her final journey:

Black is Not for Old People

"Black is not for old people.
Brown is not for old people."
On her 80th birthday, she tells her grandson,
"I'm going to go backwards from now on,
I'll be 79 next year."

"When I'm old," she announces,
"I'm not going to those senior day care places
To crochet, play bingo, make hotpads from bottle
    caps.
That's for old people."

"When I'm old, I'm going to live near a movie
    theater
So I can watch movies instead of sitting with old
    people."
At age 85, her voice echoes:
"I must be getting old."

After Alzheimer's muted her voice
I remembered her words and added to her
    wardrobe,
Lavender, light blue, green dusters, elasticized pull-
    up pants,
Loose blouses with easy access for stiffened joints.

Nothing in brown or black.
Black and brown are not for old people.

The summons from the mortuary jolts my
    awareness:
 "Bring in a blouse for the wake and final viewing of
    her body."

A rush to the mall...chill January winds whipping
    through my hair...
She needs to be warm... She needs to be warm
Black is not for old people.
Brown is not for old people.

I look through the racks for a petite blue or
    lavender woolen coat...
Where in Hawaii will I find a lavender woolen coat?
Spent from my search, clock hands racing,
I settle for the only petite coat, in brown.
Okasan, I'm sorry, I'm sorry, I know brown is not
    for old people.
But this will keep you warm on your final journey.

I add a tiara on her head,
Sprinkle vanda orchids over her folded hands.
I hear a chuckle at her viewing.

Yellow Raincoat

This morning, wearing my yellow slicker rain-coat, I ran through cold stabbing rain from my car to the mall entrance. I was immediately met with comments from fellow walkers and security guards.

"Nice raincoat!"

"That's a beautiful yellow on you."

"Can I take a photo with you in that raincoat?"

"I wore yellow like that once when I was working for the County."

I joked, "Remember, I was last seen in a yellow raincoat should I go missing," a bit embarrassed over all the attention. Columbo never received compliments on his old trench coat.

Hear that, Pāhoa High School home economics teacher? You reminded us often so we would never forget, "You Japanese girls should never wear yellow because it's too close to your yellow skin tone. It doesn't provide any contrast."

Yellow in all shades became one of my favorite colors and has been in my wardrobe ever since age sixteen. I should have taught you, teacher, never say "Don't" to a teenager whose secret dream is to become a writer. But not having developed the sassy lip yet, I bit my tongue and didn't retort, "So you won't be wearing a white wedding dress when you get married, since white will blend in too much with your white skin? Oh, and remember, white is only for virgins." That kind of sass would have gotten me expelled, so fortunately I kept my mouth shut.

Oh, and one more thing...as Columbo would have said. Little did I know that yellow would be an issue my entire life.

Shortly after my move to Sacramento, it was at a candy shop at the mall that I experienced my first encounter with anti-Asian racism. The saleswoman asked if I had cut in line, but there was no one behind me. "How could I cut in line when there's no one behind me?" I asked the woman. "Did you ask those two gentlemen in front of me if they had cut in line?" She was silent so I repeated my question, and she mumbled, "I saw other customers looking at you." There was a freeze among the customers listening in to our exchange.

"So when people look at me, it means I cut in line?" She refused to look at me. I paid for my purchase and gave her a parting shot: "I'm soooo sorry I gave you such problems!" My only regret was not writing to the home office; maybe they would have sent me boxes of free chocolate. Maybe not.

After Pearl Harbor, I know of many Japanese who

changed their names. My college professor went from Kawasaki to Kawaski, a bit more Polish sounding. Many students wore "I Am Chinese" signs on their clothing, which would have served the opposite purpose during our COVID-19 pandemic.

In recent years, I was accosted a few times by men yelling at me to take off my mask and show my Chinese face, the cause of COVID. One day I looked in the mirror with my hat, sunglasses and mask and said, "Ah shit. I still look Asian."

Cow 1 is not Cow 2

Under the rising sun
The enemy came
Wearing my face.

After Pearl Harbor, I became the enemy
After 9/11, another enemy.
After COVID-19, another Asian enemy.

Cow 1 is not Cow 2.

Putin brutalizes Ukraine
Your Russian neighbor is not Putin.
Careful, careful, Cow 1 is not Cow 2.

My ancestors bombed Pearl Harbor,
I became Cow 1. Yet, Cow 1 is not Cow 2.
Such a simple, uncomplicated rule.

Author's Note: Cow 1 is not Cow 2 is a simple concept semanticist S.I. Hayakawa once demonstrated in one of his classes. You drive along the country road, and you see a cow. Further down the road you see another cow. That first cow you saw is not the second cow. Cow 1 is not Cow 2: A more detailed explanation is found in my earlier book *Can I Have Your Pearl Bracelet?*

Live and Learn and Learn

A young father, pushing his son in a stroller, reminded me never to assume all parents want their children to attend college. Nor do all children want to attend college.

The child, about six months old, gazed up at me, smiled and babbled happily. Father agreed he has a very smart baby. When I told him he has to start saving for a college fund, he said as he rocked his body in rhythm, "Naah, he's going to be a musician."

How could I have forgotten what I had once told the Third Circuit judge in Hawai'i? After reading how he lectured the juveniles who appeared before him, admonishing them to raise their grades so they could attend college, I wrote a letter accusing him of being an elitist. What if some of the young people wanted to be the best waiter or bus driver? Think of all the people who serve him daily, from cashiers to limo drivers. He listened, invited me to lunch and thereafter sent the young offenders out to do community service, without the college prep lecture.

There are extremes, of course, like the father of a third-grade student who ignored my concern about his daughter's lack of interest in learning and said, "She's going to be Miss Hawai'i someday. All she needs to do is be a good hula dancer."

So far 2025 has been a difficult year for relationships, given the diversity of political views among us. After the election I inadvertently told a fellow walker friend, "Oh no, you're not one of those idiots..." He told me I must stop listening to lies and it's time all immigrants were deported. I wanted to point to our workers at the mall and say, "You don't mind seeing them deported?" Instead I said, "We're both listening to different news media. Look, we can't discuss politics, let's just be friends."

Years ago, I was in a similar situation in Columbus, Ohio. A pen pal's mother invited me to her home to meet her friends. Over lunch, the N-word was casually dropped into their conversations, so I interrupted, "I'm wondering why I'm here when I'm not white." They simultaneously said, "Oh, but you're not Black." I knew then that racism was here to stay because just as they would not be able to change me into one of them, I would be unable to change their minds. Only in the classroom have I been successful in bringing about these changes.

How do we maintain friendships when we differ so much in basic beliefs about, for example, climate change and the humanities? What can we do, but try to rise above differences, respect the rights of others to their own views and opinions, and return to what is friendship among mall walkers? This does not mean turning our backs when these differences cause human suffering.

There is a particular religious group that I have avoided at the mall. I'm reminded of a friend, a member of this group, who was not allowed to attend her own mother's funeral service in a Buddhist church. My friend stood outside the church throughout the entire service, unable to disobey her group's inflexible rules.

In retrospect, this religious group did help me become the kind of creative teacher needed by my students. Students of this religion were not allowed to attend classroom parties, so they were sent to the school library instead. I managed to rename the celebrations "Book Events" and turned holiday parties into educational gatherings where students shared their written stories and poetry followed by refreshments. One year, after a social studies unit on different cultures, we held an international luncheon with parents while other classes were having their holiday celebrations. It takes a little creativity to do the right thing and teach outside the box when religion interferes with the education of our children.

The mall is a microcosm of the outside world, with just as many complexities and just as many opportunities for learning. I've been taught some valuable life lessons at the mall, by the most unexpected people: children, the elderly, strangers and even the homeless.

I learned empathy from a homeless man during the height of the pandemic. On one specific walk toward the mall, a homeless man asked me for my mask. After I told him I didn't have a spare, he approached me with hands out, ready to take the mask off my face. I ran off toward the mall. I heard him yelling, "God is going to punish you." He must have been just as afraid of COVID as I was, and knew the mask was protection.

Since that day, I keep cash and a mask in ziplock bags for the homeless. One December day I saw a homeless man sitting in the cold, in front of the post office. He looked at the ziplock bag I handed him, turned to me and said, "This is a lot of money for me, and this is a lot of money for you, too. God bless you." He undid the earlier curse bestowed upon me by the other homeless person.

How very true indeed, I thought. Whatever we do to others, we do to ourselves.

Whatever We Do to Others, We Do to Ourselves

At the post office this morning, I waited in line about fifteen minutes for my turn. On my way out, I opened the door for a couple with walkers. They had packages in their walker baskets, but they were leaving because of the long line. I offered to wait in line for them while they sat in the car. The man declined my offer, while his wife looked at me with a smile. I felt she wanted to accept my offer.

They needed address labels so they could mail their packages elsewhere, somewhere with a shorter line. I noticed the packages weren't addressed and thought of writing the address for them, but I respected the husband's wish to be independent. So I returned to the counter and in a very loud voice that made people in line look at me, told the clerk, "There are two handicapped people out there. I offered to wait in line for them, but all they want are address labels, which I can't find anywhere. Do you have address labels?"

One postal clerk brushed me off with, "We don't have any." Another said, "We have them," and she handed me a stack. By then the elderly man had entered, saying he couldn't stand in line and just wanted some labels.

When I gave him the stack, his wife tearfully thanked me for my kindness. I touched her hand and wished her a good holiday. In my world, anyone first in line would have given their space to the couple.

Yesterday, I went to a hospital for a test. I had printed instructions telling me I would be escorted from the Information Desk to Pulmonary because of its complicated location. The man at Info told me abruptly, "No one's here, just go left and right." I took my pen out and said, "I'm instructed to have an escort, but I will write your directions down." He rudely repeated, "Just go left and right." Someone working nearby offered to escort me there, but thanks to poor signage in the long hallways, she became confused and didn't know which elevator to take.

Then another worker, a pulmonary technician, offered to guide me. We had an interesting conversation along the way, and I ended up agreeing to speak at the hospital's conference on compassion in the workplace next September. This technician graciously escorted me all the way back to the entrance after my test.

In my world, people who work with patients wouldn't need such a conference on compassion—being compassionate would be a job requirement, and displaying a lack of it would be grounds for dismissal.

Caregivers understand well "what we do to others, we do to ourselves." When we show disrespect toward our loved ones, we are disrespecting ourselves. When we treat our loved ones with dignity, we are dignifying ourselves. A caregiver didn't like herself because she was yelling at her mother for asking the same question over and over again. "I'm not a good person," she repeated. "I don't like myself."

"Can you enter her world?" I suggested. "In her world, she is asking that question for the first time. Think you can answer it as though she is asking it for the first time?" This became a turning point, and she began to discover how capable she was in caring for her mother with less yelling. I did tell her to go yell at a tree if she needs to yell. Yelling at a human being creates self-punishment. Whatever we do to others, be it kindness or rudeness, will be reflected back upon us.

The Path Taken

What other path is there
Except for the divine
Where love, kindness, compassion
Help me discover little pieces of myself
That make me smile,
Bringing me such quiet joy
At the end of the day.
After she is gone,
The gift she gave me of myself
Will bring me such sadness
But lasting peace.

CONVERSATIONS WITH MR. H

I first saw him on Howe Avenue near the mall. He had staked his new home beside a business complex, on a strip of property between the shrubs that concealed the entrance to the building and the street. He must be a minimalist, I decided, since he didn't have a cart or a single garbage bag; perhaps he's newly homeless.

"Ah, Mr. H. That's good. Keep it clean. You are still here after a week. If you respect that property under you, I'm sure they will let you stay."

Each time I passed Mr. H. I felt moved by the business establishment's kindness. Was an emergency conference called to debate on this new addition to their entrance? Was it a problem that needed action? I envisioned an animated discussion:

"Look, he's not doing any harm. He's keeping the area clean. Seems like a responsible guy."

"He's been here three weeks now, and we haven't had any complaints from our customers."

"I noticed some of our customers are stopping by to talk story with him. He's receiving food and cash."

"Since he's keeping the place clean, how about we let him stay?"

And they did.

A month later, empty soda cans began to appear, strewn around his few belongings. Plastic bags were tossed by the wind and smashed under passing cars. Piles of garbage were growing like giant amoebae. His single-occupancy home now housed three.

"Oh no, Mr. H. This is not good. You gotta keep it clean or they won't let you stay. Tell your friends they need to respect that property and the business folks who are letting you stay.

"You gotta teach your friends about respect, dignity and responsibility. See if this makes sense. We are all residents of this planet and when we are given the privilege of living on this planet, we do our best to take care of it, not only for ourselves but for everyone else. This is called 'Being part of humanity.' I hope there's telepathy between us, Mr. H, because I'm afraid you're destroying your own home."

Unfortunately, ESP was not working for either of us. Just as I anticipated, construction tools and machinery soon appeared. Within a few hours, skeletons of a gate and fence emerged. Within days, a new gate and fence stood. The residents were gone.

"Mr. H, wherever you are, I hope you know what happened. It wasn't the folks at the business where you had staked your home who removed your shelter. I think it was your failure to respect their property.

"This lifestyle that ignores the greater community is not confined to the homeless, so I'm not targeting you alone. At a health gym where I was a member, strands of hair were left in the porcelain sinks, toilets were left unflushed, tissues and toilet paper dotted the floors. Someone had failed these folks, too. Parents or teachers had not taught them about cleaning up after themselves. And they were not homeless. No, they came from their homes to start the day at the gym, dressed in their blazers and skirts after a hot shower, and left to go to work. But unlike yours, Mr. H., their thoughtless behavior was kept private, and they returned to their own homes.

"So what happens, Mr. H. if you are given a real roof over your head? Even as I write this, blueprints are being drawn at the city and state level. Will you take ownership and live by respecting every part of that house as though you had built it yourself? Will you work in a vegetable garden to help provide food for yourself? Or even become a self-employed gardener? Will you help others understand the importance of all these words I've been tossing out to you: ownership, responsibility, dignity, respect and gratitude?

"I hope those who build you a shelter also know that the solution to the homeless is not only about getting a roof over your heads. A house whose residents are not committed to maintaining it will eventually self-destruct. A house without feeling your own human worth will remain just a roof over your head, not a home.

"This is what families do: they take pride in their home's appearance, inside and out; they cook nutritious meals, they share household chores, they work in their vegetable gardens. They get to know and respect their neighbors, whom they help by teaching what they have learned. We call this paying it forward or living with *omoiyari*—thinking of others first. Being part of a community means more than just having a shelter, Mr. H.

"You may have abilities and talents that are needed by our community, by our elders, by our young. Those who give you a shelter must see you as a human being, not just a homeless person. I know you have stories to tell and experiences from which all of us, children and adults alike, could benefit. Hey, maybe you could host a community event where I help everyone write some poetry and stories. Wouldn't that be something? You could even become published. Maybe you will build a stage or community center where you can hold poetry readings, musical concerts, and art displays; or where YOU could lead workshops for others. I know you will be of great value to the children. It's the arts that will nurture our shared humanity. It is already happening, Mr. H.

"It's a privilege when others reach out to you, and I so want you to feel this pride of being a responsible person. I so want you to be part of our community. It's a good feeling, Mr. H., to live with dignity and gratitude and to know you are making a difference. Once you forget this, you may find yourself living on the side of a street again and again."

I'm not naïve enough to think that my words here can eradicate homelessness. Yes, it's a multi-faceted and complex problem. But maybe, maybe, if we begin with one, we may get somewhere. I wish you well, Mr. H.

JANUARY 20, 2025

I was five years old when Pearl Harbor was bombed on December 7, 1941. I sensed then that we had a dangerous enemy, and that enemy was me:

> under the rising sun
> the enemy came
> wearing my face.

I was too young to understand why rice was often replaced by pasta. All things Japanese were buried in the backyard: medicine bottles, books, family heirlooms, photos. The doors to the Japanese language school were locked. A friend's father, a Japanese language teacher, was deported to an internment camp. "Speak English, even to your grandparents," became our new mantra. For my safety, I needed to become "American" and bury my heritage. I am American, but sadly my face was still the face of the enemy. A woman from the village told me years later that she was sent to the internment camp, but her children were never told this. "I don't want my children's love and respect for their country tarnished by how their mother and grandparents were treated."

Today I encountered Pearl Harbor by another name at the mall where I do my morning walks. Bella is a cleaning woman there. For years, she and I have exchanged greetings in her native language, Spanish.

Buenos dias, Bella, como esta hoy?

Bien, bien. Bella takes pride in being able to tell her fellow workers that she is my "Spanish teacher." I'm not the best student, but over the year my vocabulary has grown, our lessons now include hugs and warm exchanges.

Today during the presidential inauguration, I saw a different Bella. Her black hair was now streaked with bright highlights. Her normally plain and beautiful face was painted with eye shadow and lipstick. Before I could greet her, she approached me with, "Good morning. How are you?" in perfect English.

I took the cue and greeted her back in English. It was Pearl Harbor all over again. No one saw the grief under my COVID mask as I finished my walk and whispered, "Adios, mi amiga" to Bella.

I am America.

Forgive me for who I have become.
My arms no longer embrace all people.
My feet tread on the poor.
My eyes are blinded by stupidity, ignorance, greed.
My heart, frozen by fiery lust.
My ears, deafened by hate.
My soul blackened by evil and greed,
Envy of those knowing love.

Bury me now for my rebirth
As the America I was meant to be.

You Know Who You Are

Forgive the people
Who made you who you are.
You have no tears
For the dying poor in Africa, or
In your neighborhood.
Dollar signs have replaced
Compassion, kindness and joy.
Forests destroyed for real estate
Give you more meaning
When there is more life in trees
Than any condo can sell or rent.
Forgive those who made you
Who you have become.
To not know what it means
To be human is the unforgivable.
To not know love and kindness
Are the saddest inheritance
Given to anyone.
May your child be spared
What was done to you.

THE MALL SCROOGE

Dean (Martin) stopped me at the mall and asked, "How is the emperor's daughter this morning?" I looked at him, pleased as any author would be when a reader appears. I said, "You read my *Echoes of Kapoho* book."

"Yes," he said. "I pick up your Kapoho book often. Those stories lift my spirit. When you were growing up in Kapoho, you dreamed of being at cocktail parties in New York City and Paris, and here you are, walking the mall with the rest of us. I read your Christmas poem again, and I can recite the last four lines for you."

A Kapoho Christmas

It was Christmas without lights.
It was Christmas without indoor plumbing.
It was Christmas without carolers at the window
Muffed and warm under falling snow.

But there was Christmas.

A Christmas program at school
The Holy Night reenacted:
White tissue paper glued on coconut fronds
Shaped as angel wings and haloes.
Long white robes over bare feet.

The plantation manager with bags of hard candies,
His annual role in the village where he reigned.
Fathers in Sunday best
After a hard day's work in sugar cane fields.
Mothers in home-sewn dresses
Inspired by Sears catalog photos.
Children, restless, on wooden benches,
Waiting for Santa's jolly Ho Ho Ho.

A fir tree from the hills,
Needles not lasting 24 hours.
Colored construction-paper chains,
Origami ornaments and tin-foiled tinsel.
Gas and kerosene lamps
Moving shadows on the walls.

It was not the Christmas of my dreams.
No one singing Silent Night, Holy Night.
No large presents under a real Christmas tree.
No fireplaces with rooftop chimneys.
No blue-eyed boy handing me hot chocolate.

For 18 years, my fantasy Christmas
Existed in my head...until Fire Goddess Pele
Came to my rescue from Kīlauea Crater
And covered our whole village.

Finally! I said, without a backward glance,
Running out fast in bare feet
Along unpaved roads
To the Christmas of my dreams.

We stood as he recited the last stanza.

"And I never had that Christmas," I said. He nodded, adding, "We often don't."

No, my deep desire to have that perfect Christmas was for the child I once was. Sometimes we need to grow up to discover the real Christmas. Living in remote Kapoho on Hawai'i's Big Island, looking at magazine ads of costly picture-perfect Christmases left me dissatisfied with Kapoho Christmas. As an adult, the Christmas of my dreams has undergone quite a change.

Today I'm Christmas Scrooge, disgusted with TV ads and shop displays that turn Christmas into a commercial shopping festival. Children are indoctrinated to believe there can be no real Christmas without lots of presents and extravagant decorations.

In my classroom, it was always a Kapoho Christmas. "Any tree can become a Christmas tree," I said, and brought in a guava tree branch from the yard, decorating it as we did in Kapoho with homemade ornaments. I knew many a child's only gift was one from the Salvation Army; they were looking at Christmas, from the outside.

Somewhere

Somewhere a child is looking in, as I did,
At Christmas as it ought to be:
Lighted fir tree, presents, carolers at the door,
Snowflakes and Santa Claus with bundles of toys.

Somewhere a 16-year-old is looking in, as I did,
At two lovers with wine-filled crystal goblets,
Cozy beside a crackling fire, exchanging gifts.
Somewhere a parent is looking in
At the Christmas she wishes to give her child,
Seeing bank ads for loans flash on the TV screen,
Knowing she won't qualify, won't find the cash
It takes to make Christmas right.

Somewhere else, a child is drawn to the sound of
    bells
And puts his last dime in the red kettle.
Somewhere a child visits the forgotten in nursing
    homes
And shares lopsided cookies, her homemade
Stars and trees sprinkled with red and green.
Somewhere a child hands a loaf of warm bread
And a cup of cocoa to a homeless person
Who blesses the child.
Somewhere...

I mailed this to the North Pole a few days ago:

Dear Santa,

I'm not here to question your existence
Nor am I here to claim I've been good,
Just a question or two about your annual visit.
You've been ho-ho-ho-ing for eons now, toting
Bags that get bulkier and heavier each coming year.

Once upon a time, you carried oranges,
Homemade Raggedy Ann dolls, cars carved
Out of fallen oak branches, blank sheets of paper,
Boxes of crayons, pens, and books.
Ah yes, books.
Remember, Santa?

There were no televisions screaming
Buy, Buy, Buy,
No ads from banks, wheedling
Borrow, Borrow, Borrow,
Hiding the high interest payments,
That would appear after the holidays.

I want, I want, I want is now the norm
From children sitting on your lap.

Remember when strings of popcorn
Draped the trees and carolers filled the air?
Remember when children listened to their parents
Instead of their handheld electronic devices?
And giving was more important than receiving?

So tell me Santa,
Did all those toys that would soon be broken...
Broken like so many human spirits,
Did giving these bring YOU any joy?
Your bag of stuff, Santa,
Distorts the meaning of Christmas
Into things, things, things.

Tell me Santa, why don't you visit
All children, rich, poor and homeless?
Your bag is already too heavy, you say?

I know a way Santa, to lighten your load,
If you'll give me a minute or two.
Find some elves in your workshop up North,
Elves on the poetic side, perhaps. Hand them
Nothing but a pencil and sheets of blank sheets.

"Imagine," tell them, "Imagine gifts that are not
    material,
Like Kindness, Compassion, Gratitude,
And yes, even Color Blindness, gifts that will
Humanize all children listening for our sleigh
    bells."

Then perhaps someday your bag will be weightless,
Filled with the true gifts of Christmas
That will last all year and into adulthood.
Trust me, Santa, your HO-HO-HO
Will even carry a different tune.

I wish I were one of Santa's elves to help lighten Santa's
sleigh.

It's Opium in 2024

Holidays can become times of grief and pain, remembering those who are no longer with us. But we still have the option to select the best of memories to see us through the holidays. My friend Charlie Pellegrino, who lost family in the North Tower on 9/11, shared with me a comforting thought that noted science-fiction writer Arthur C. Clarke wrote to him in a letter not long after: "Remember that you knew them, not that you lost them." The following memory has helped me all these years, bringing a chuckle and a smile instead of grieving for my mother who is now gone.

I bought Opium perfume today, a gift from my mother who has been gone for twenty –two years. She owes me $119.61.

It was a Christmas tradition between us, a tradition that filled the living room with laughter and joy, created by a manipulative daughter.

Since college, I had returned home to my mother's every holiday. Our annual December conversation never changed. After showing my mother an outfit or a piece of jewelry, I would say, "Hey Okasan, do you want to buy me this for my Christmas gift this year?"

Okasan: Sure, how much?

Me: Only $$$.

No matter what price I quoted, her response was always the same:

"Only that much and you can't pay for yourself?"

And she would hand me a hundred-dollar bill saying, "Aren't you shamed to take money from your poor mother when you have a good job?"

I always pulled the money out of her hand and said, "No, no shame."

Her laughter would spark, and it was a time of joy between mother and daughter, an indirect way of acknowledging our relationship, a relationship in a culture where expressing love with hugs and words was awkward.

After she was diagnosed with Alzheimer's and since her death in 2002, our Christmas tradition continued in silence: Every Christmas I have bought a gift from her to me. Today she gave me a bottle of my favorite perfume, Opium.

The perfume shop salesman listened to my story while I made the purchase. The poor man, I thought, forced to hear stories from customers to help make a sale. When he handed me the perfume, I saw deep emotion in his eyes as though he were fighting back tears. He said, "So this Opium is for you from your mother up there" and he turned his eyes toward the ceiling.

I nodded, "Yes." And he said, "She heard every word you said to me. She is smiling down at you."

As I thanked him and left, the fragrance of Opium from the sample sprayed on my hand followed me out the shop. "Hey, Okasan," I said silently, dodging shoppers in the mall, "You owe me $119.61."

The Christmas Spirit

It's not the best of times, it's not the worst of times, it's just been a bad year: pink slips ten days before Christmas, flickers of uncertainty and fear on faces in public places. In a supermarket aisle, a woman who looked like a kindly cookie-baking grandmother snarled at me, "Watch it!" when my cart got too close to hers. Dumbfounded, I quickly gave her space.

In line at the post office, I heard a menacing voice growl to an elderly man, "You're standing too close to me. People like you shouldn't be allowed in public." The closer we get to Christmas the more distance we seem to need from each other.

Yesterday when I entered a furniture store, the full contingent of salespeople swooped toward me like predatory birds. Did they smell cash in my pocket? I wanted to hide my leather coat.

"Thank you, I'm just looking," I repeated, and walked toward the room displays. When another customer entered, a salesman was on the man in an instant. "May I help you?" The man replied, "I just want a place to sit."

I glanced his way again, and he didn't look like cash to me. He was unshaven, skin sallow. A thin, shabby coat hung loose on his gaunt frame. He looked like a refugee from Loaves & Fishes, definitely out of his element. I braced myself for the confrontation that I knew was coming and prepared to run defense for the man. The salesman looked him over, then gestured to a collection of pricey sofas.

"Be my guest," he said softly. Then as an afterthought, "Just be careful not to get the furniture wet." He walked away.

I didn't buy anything that visit. But when I do have cash for furniture, you can be sure I'll return and find that compassionate salesman. In this bleak 2024 holiday season, he is the only one I encountered who demonstrated the true Spirit of Christmas: peace on Earth, goodwill to men.

Ban Banned Books

*S*ave *Democracy! Read Banned Books!* This sign appeared in the window of a dress shop at the mall, with a display of banned books interspersed among the dresses on sale. Some of the titles I spotted were *Charlotte's Web*, *Strega Nona*, *Bridge to Terabithia* and *The Witches*. I was deeply moved by the sight and silently applauded the shop's courage.

Looking back, I have some unpleasant memories associated with book banning. When I was sixteen years old, high school faculty would not allow me to borrow library books without teacher approval. They suspected I was reading books that were too advanced and contained sexually explicit material. They were mistaken. In fact, the book I was seen reading, *Office Wife*, would be found in the Young Adults section of any library or bookstore today. That requirement to have all my reading material approved felt not only constraining but shaming, and as a result I became a staunch advocate of reading freedom for all.

At the mall that day, I donated a check to the shop to be spent on more banned books. It's easy to write a check; I wanted to do more, so I called upon my literary mouse friend, Wordsworth the Poet. I walked for days, thinking of how Wordsworth and his friends could approach banned books.

I may have passed the mall walkers, ignoring their greetings or hand waves for weeks. I was thinking. When I was in my thirties, Saturday was my day of relaxation from teaching five days a week in Hilo on the Big Island of Hawai'i, and I would walk downtown, looking in dress shops and having a leisurely lunch. One Saturday, my mother was waiting on the porch and I sensed she had waited all afternoon for the sound of my car driving up the gravel road to the garage. I was hardly in the house when she told me what she'd been waiting to tell me.

"Hideko!" she said laughingly, "Do you know you passed your own mother on the sidewalk in front of Kress Store? Your own mother. Da nerve, passing your own mother!"

"I did?" I laughingly asked. "Oh, I was thinking."

I was thinking again at the mall when I found Wordsworth at the beach, enjoying the quiet sound...

Wordsworth:
> I was sitting at the beach, enjoying the quiet
> sound of the waves splashing on shore, thinking
> of another poem to write, when my friends Akiko,
> Eliot and Dylan—and even Frances!—turned my
> morning into a day of loud dialogue about book
> banning. Did you know in many parts of our
> country, people are not allowed to read certain
> books or even say certain words? Will they ban my
> books next? Here are my friends interrupting my
> silence.

Eliot:

Wordsworth! Wordsworth!
I can't find *Huckleberry Finn*
And *Bridge to Terabithia!*
My two favorite books are missing!

Wordsworth:

Slow down, Eliot
Go to the library.
Books are always there.

Eliot:

No! No!
Look at that truck!
They're taking all the books away!
There's *Huck Finn* and *Charlotte's Web!*

Akiko:

They said those books are bad for us.
They said it's for our own good.
They don't want us to know
How to think and grow.

Eliot:

Who are they?
Why are they banning books?
Where did they come from?
Do they know more than we do?

Dylan:

They are adults! Adults!
They were children once.
Did books do them wrong?

Eliot:

I don't know.
They don't want us to know.
They don't want us to see.
They don't want us to think.
They don't want us to feel.
They don't want us to grow.

Akiko:

How will we know what we don't know?
How will we know what's right and not right?
How will we know truth from lies
If we are left in cages, without books?

Dylan:

Wordsworth! Do something!
Are you writing a poem?
What good will a poem do
When trucks are emptying library shelves?

Wordsworth:

Why? Why?
Books are made of words,
Not of guns and daggers and swords.
Like wings of birds
They fly us to worlds beyond...
Beyond our imagination
To places unknown.
All the words in books,
In our dictionary they dwell.
Why are they so afraid of words?

Oh, what glory they spell.
Will they ban dictionaries next?
"Gay" is forbidden in classrooms.
Will they ban our teacher Miss Gay?

Dylan:
Wordsworth!
You can't use gay
In your poems.
They will ban your books.
Why are you not afraid?

Wordsworth:
In many places
Including ours,
Poets are feared
More than knives and swords.
When a poet
Puts pen to paper
There is hope for peace
And freedom and truth
So a poet's pen, my friends
Is what we will use
Till the banning ends.

Akiko:
What can we do?
Write poems, Wordsworth,
And post them on walls
Of bookshops and libraries,
Supermarkets, too?

Maybe to the governor!
And to the President!

Eliot:
Yes. Yes.
Put them in a book, Wordsworth,
So every reader will help us
Unban our banned books.
Ban Banning Books.
Alliteration, Wordsworth.
Use this title for your book!

Wordsworth:
Great title, Eliot.
I can't do this job alone.
We all need to do this together
If we want to free our books
And put them back where they belong.
On our library shelves!

Akiko, Dylan, Eliot:
Oh look! Frances is here!

Frances:
Maybe I can help.
I wrote this poem about librarians.
What do you think?

In Praise of Librarians

No Nobel Prize for what you do,
Librarians, no trip to Sweden,

No medals, gold, silver or bronze.
But you deserve our thanks and praise
For preserving the words that record
Our history and our knowledge;
Our stories, songs and poems;
Our thoughts, feelings, hopes and ideas.
Our shared humanity is in your keeping.

Hardly noticed among the Dewey decimals
You stand, fearless and tireless, against
The harsh winds of ignorance,
The bonfires of censorship,
The wordless acts of forgetting
How we became who we are.

You educate, challenge and inspire
Children of all ages, opening to them
The world of written words,
Just as you did when I was a little girl
Gobbling up all the words you handed me.

Those words are your legacy
To future generations,
So, thank you, Librarians, keepers
Of the books in which we live.

Wordsworth:
>	Yes. Yes.
>	SOS! Librarians!
>	Nurturers of children's minds.

Help us turn back the trucks
Hauling books off your shelves.
Give us a podium to read our poems.
Let our pens and voices
Be the new sound of freedom!

Dylan:
Wait! Wait!
I want to hitchhike on those trucks
And read all those books banned from us.
I can read, I can think, I can imagine.
Don't take those books away from me.
I want to know why they're banned.
Let me decide if words turn into swords and
    knives.
Let me decide, not them.

Akiko:
Yes. Yes.
Let's meet at the library every Saturday,
Read all the books that have been banned,
All those words they want hidden:
Words about a spider that can spell,
Or a friend who loses a friend,
Words like Witch from Roald Dahl
And simple words that teach us
Why we must not hate,
Why it's OK to be different,
How to be kind to all creatures,
How to care for our planet.
Let's read all those books

And decide for ourselves
What makes sense!

Wordsworth:
Yes!
Children everywhere.
Meet at your library
Or in your special tree house
Or under your porch.
Here's to the Ban Banned Books Book Club of
    Children everywhere.
Read them, check them, compare them,
Learn from them!
Make up your own mind!

Akiko, Dylan, Eliot:
Wordsworth! Frances!
They may ban your books
But fear not.
To the Supreme Court
We will go.
Children everywhere
Will return them to shelves
The whole world over.

We will go to our libraries.
We will march to our bookstores.
We will rescue our books
And put them back where they belong.
Where we can read them,
Where we can learn from them,

Where we can discover
What the world is really like
So we can know how to make it better.
Better, better, better.
Free our books,
Keep our minds free.

Wordsworth:
Let's write our poems,
Our stories, too.
We're stronger than "they" are.
To the library! To the Dictionary!
Read banned books.
Read your poems.
Our words to freedom!

Wordsworth, Akiko, Dylan, Eliot, Frances:
Turn on the lights!
Turn on the lights!
To basements where
Banned books dwell.
Read banned books!
Turn on the lights.
To poets and writers.
Your given rights,
Loud and clear.
Sing out your voice.
Turn on the lights.
Turn on the lights.

THANK YOU, POETS FOR CHANGE

I thank you on behalf of all the children
Of the world. Your children,
Your children for change.

The voice of the poet
Is stronger than bullets, stronger than bombs
That send black ashes into our skies,
Stronger than tyrants armed with false promises.

The voice of the poet
Is stronger than Hate or Greed,
Destroyers of our planet Earth.

Thank you, poets, for your voice today.
Soon, these questions won't need to be asked:
What is love? What is Peace? What is a world
        without war?
Thank you, poets, for our planet,
Of safe foods, pure air and water.
Soon no dictionary will we need
To define each word in our Constitution.
We will be living those words, because of you.
We will all hold hands and respect
All colors, races, religions, genders and ages
And all species, too.
Thank you, Poets.

A Kapoho Childhood

Backward, turn backward, O Time, in your flight,
Make me a child again, just for tonight!...
...give me my childhood again!

– Elizabeth Akers Allen
1832-1911

My thoughts return to Kapoho, watching children skipping in the mall, stopping to look at store displays.

I was that free-spirited child, visiting people's homes without invitation, dropping in on one house where I knew Fanny would offer me warm Pepsi in a white mug, or on to another house when I knew Beth would be cooking dinner, listening in on conversations. I was a regular visitor to Beth's kitchen when she was cooking her oxtail soup. Beth's father and brother unintentionally stigmatized her family when they were deported to the Moloka'i leper colony; people became wary of eating food she prepared. It was a hush-hush conversation among the villagers, but Beth openly talked to me about what they were saying. She told me how once a year, the airlines flew her father and brother to the Hilo airport, where Beth and her family would stand and watch the airplane land. They would wave to their father and brother through the airplane windows, and after a few minutes of waving, the plane would return to Moloka'i. That was the only way her father and brother would be allowed to leave Moloka'i. Beth made the best oxtail soup and told the best ghost stories.

An elderly Hawaiian woman to whose house I invited myself, usually during mealtime, gave me a piece of advice that I failed to follow. "When you get married," she said, "never put your wedding picture in the newspaper." Weddings were a big deal, and photos of the new couple were often published in the *Hilo Tribune Herald*. "If you put your picture in the newspaper, somebody somewhere is going to wipe their ass with your face."

Yes, in Kapoho, most families used the *Hilo Tribune Herald*, the Sears and Montgomery Ward catalogs as our Charmin. In most outhouses, square sheets of these publications dangled from a nail on the wall, our Charmin, at arm's reach. The Kakugawa outhouse had a box of apple wrappers in a used apple box in one corner, wrappers sent to us from a relative who had a grocery store in Hilo. Years later, I recognized the feel of apple wrappers in the bathrooms in England. I wrote in my journal, "No wonder the Queen always looks constipated, their toilet paper feels like apple wrappers."

My first news photo appeared in the *Hilo Tribune Herald* when I was a senior in high school; I had received a scholarship from the University of Hawai'i alumni. Did I subsequently become a sheet of Charmin? I have an image of that Hawaiian woman tsk-tsking, "I told her not to put her face in the paper. She should have listened to me."

I eavesdropped a lot on people's conversations and one statement from an *issei* neighbor who was the first in the village to receive U.S. citizenship still resonates today.

Henry, a nintey-year-old immigrant from Japan, related the best hospital story ever. He was in for surgery, and when awakened by the night shift nurse to take a painkiller, he refused, saying,

"No need painkiller. Why you wake me up from sleep?" When the nurse explained it was the doctor's orders, Henry shouted, "Me Body, Me Boss!" Then he turned around to return to sleep.

When the DMV refused to renew his driver's license, as requested by his son because of his father's age, Henry retorted, "I pay taxes, I'm American citizen, I have rights." The DMV listened, and his license was renewed. Individual voices were heard in those days.

One uncle often told me, a scrawny girl wearing loose home-made dresses to conceal her legs covered with Band-Aids over impetigo, "Someday you are going to be a beautiful woman." This may have fueled my dream of becoming a glamorous Hollywood star. My uncle didn't turn out to be a seer.

There must have been dozens of eyes watching the Kakugawa girl protectively, kind neighbors hoping she would someday take her Kapoho survival skills out in the wider world she sought.

Once There Was a Kapoho

Once there was a Kapoho

Where barefooted children played
until the evening sun disappeared
and gas and kerosene lamplight
beckoned each child home.

Once there was a Kapoho

where outhouses and water tanks
stood like proud sentinels
and ʻōhiʻa firewood sent signals
above rooftops, announcing
a hot *furo* for weary workers.

Once there was a Kapoho

where mothers pumped away
on manual sewing machines,
making clothes and one-strap schoolbags

for the first of September
marking the end of summer.

Once there was a Kapoho

without television,
where battery-run radios
crackled *The Romance of Helen Trent,
Dr. Malone* and *Arthur Godfrey.*

Once there was a Kapoho

with wooden washboards
and concrete tubs
instead of washing machines,
where slippery, muddy denims
were soaked in Saloon Pilot cans.

Once there was a place

without shopping malls and Macy's,
where mail-order catalogs were dream makers,
a place so simple and free.
where children swam in Warm Springs
and fished in Green Lake,
played marbles and Ojame
and Steal Steal Stone.

Once there was a place

where life was lived without question,
sons went off to war,

teachers taught the three Rs,
parents attended PTA meetings,
and children pledged allegiance.

Yes, once there was such a place
until Madam Pele said, "No more!"
and scattered all the children
like stars across the universe,
echoing Thomas Wolfe,
"You can't go home again."

Author's Notes:

issei: first-generation Japanese

furo: wooden bathtub

Madame Pele: Hawaiian goddess of fire, who dwells in
Kīlauea Crater

WANTED: A NEW MIRROR

How did this happen? I woke up in 2025 and saw my mother's face in the mirror. How did this happen? How did I become so old? When I was sixty-nine, I wrote the following two poems, believing eighty-eight was forever away.

On Becoming 69

How can I be 69 when I feel 49?
How can my mother's daughter turn 69?
For God's sake, children aren't supposed to age.
How can my mother's daughter turn 69?
They began mailing me funeral plans,
Nursing home ads in glossy color brochures
In large black print.
They gave me flu shots before anyone else,
Invitations to free luncheons
By long-term care insurance agents.
"You are dying," their messages said.
They probably hadn't heard of my 88th birthday,
When I plan to make love and hear the leaves move
On a windless day.

When I Am 88

When I am 88
I will have a love affair
That will leave me trembling
On a windless day.
I will drown in Puccini,
Mozart, Verdi.
Tidal waves roaring
Inside of me.
I will feel the brush strokes
Of van Gogh,
Clawing, bleeding
My inner flesh.
I will be Shakespeare
Vibrant, on stage,
Rivers rushing, splashing
Over moss and stone.
I will become soft,
Sensuous, wet
Against your skin,
Silk against steel.
When I am 88
I will still be woman,
Yes!

My eighty-eighth year has come and gone. How do I live when travel is no longer a stress-free adventure? I no longer drive the freeway to explore cities two hours away. I can no longer take a full swing with that golf club. I gave up golf anyway, after becoming a caregiver for my mother who had Alzheimer's disease. My flute is stored away, as I can no longer hold my breath for over a minute. It's time for Plan B: Accept it and live with it gracefully. Two friends taught me the first item under Plan B. "Stop dyeing your hair; silvery white hair at your age is dignified. Nothing is worse than an old woman trying to look young!"

Plan B had an auspicious beginning:

Going silver takes a bit of orientation and re-training of the creative mind. When the X-ray technician told me what an excellent patient I had been and walked me to the exit door, I knew he had seen something in the X-rays and suspected I had a few months or weeks to live. When the MRI technician did the same, walking me out to my car in the parking lot, wishing me a beautiful rest of the day, I knew I was dying. Otherwise, why all this kindness?

OMG.

I must be dying.
Why all this kindness
Unless I'm dying?

After my CT scan, the technician
Walked me out of the hospital,
Right to the parking lot.
His kindness was suspect.

Today the MRI technician
Took my hand and said,
"You are the best patient ever."
OMG. Another act of kindness.
Or was he impressed I could hold my breath
For 30 seconds while the tube
Machine gunned me for 40 minutes?

His, "Excellent, Frances," echoed
Through antiseptic halls as we walked,
His arm around me, to the exit.
I'm dying. I'm dying.

What brought me here,
Suspicious and distrusting
Simple human kindness
OMG!
Maybe they thought I was
Hot and attractive. Why not?
Or were they merely being
Kind to the dying?

The Uninvited Guest

At a certain stage in life, usually called the Golden Years, an uninvited guest enters the house and simply refuses to leave, settling in as a permanent resident. Called Elf or Leprechaun or Somebody. In our house he is the Menehune, a legendary Hawaiian trickster. Sometimes he follows me to the mall or to grocery stores without my knowing.

He hides reading glasses, car keys, pens, medication, books, even mugs of coffee. He could trick Penn and Teller for sure. He even plays with minds. Have you ever entered a room and stood for a second, thinking, "Now why did I come here?" Then that frightening thought enters...that unnerving thought, "Am I losing it? Is this the start of dementia?" It's that Menehune playing his tricks again.

One day he snuck into my car as I left for the market. After shopping, I couldn't find my car key. With my left hand, I searched all my pockets, no key. I searched the "key pocket" in my handbag, the home for my keys, no key. In a state of panic, I rushed to my car hoping the key was not in the ignition. With my right hand, I reached for the car door and there was the key in my right hand. I'm ambidextrous, so that adds to the confusion.

This is when my monologue begins. "Stupid. Stupid. Next time don't take your keys out until you get to the car." I hear the chuckle from the back seat. As I know from experience, this will happen again.

He often changes dates on my calendar and embarrasses me when I arrive for a hair appointment. To my "Am I late?" the hairdresser answers, "Like yesterday." Would my doctor's receptionist understand if I told her why I had missed my appointment? "The Menehune changed the date on my calendar." To save face, I've often asked friends to change the dates on their birth certificates when a birthday card from me arrives on the wrong date.

Menehune is like an old dog; you can't teach him anything. How often have I told him to turn the stove off when I leave the kitchen, forgetting our Number One Kitchen Rule: Never leave the kitchen with the stove on. So many dinners burnt, so many pots beyond Ajax or Comet.

How this Menehune flew in all the way from Hawai'i is a mystery. Wish I knew how to get him a plane ticket back to the Islands.

RSVP

The cardiologist walked into the room with a copy of my EKG and said, "I have three patients who are one hundred years old, all in perfect health, and you are going to join them."

"You are invited to my one hundredth birthday party, Doctor," I replied.

"I'll be dead by then," he retorted.

"No," I said, "You can't die before me."

When a physician insists you have a decade more of life, thoughts and fears of death fade into the background. I walked out of the room feeling younger than springtime. So inspired, I came home and began working on this book.

Some people keep personal life events private while I broadcast mine over the coconut wireless, sharing them with friends and family. The more I speak of them, the less traumatic they become. Once when I thought I had cancer, I calmed my fears by writing and publishing poems on the What Ifs. Now when I tell you, "Hey, I'm dying," dying has become less threatening.

So, you are all invited to my Hundredth Birthday Party and do bring presents. When I extended this invitation to the Presidents' Table at the mall, the men offered, "I'll give you cash. How about a gift certificate?""No," I said. "No cash or gift cards. You need to shop long and hard to find something special for me."

John and Michaela promised me one hundred pennies. Dean promised me a pearl bracelet in honor of my book *Can I Have Your Pearl Bracelet*. I said, "Wait, my next book title will be *Can I Have Your Diamond Necklace!*" Someone asked if I would still have teeth; should he bring mashed carrots from his garden?

When I Am 100

When I am 100, my dearest,
Bring me no flannel nightgowns.
Long-sleeved with buttons up to my chin,
No house slippers lined with fleece.
No skid-free socks up to my knees.
Whoever told you old is cold
Ought to be duct taped!

Let me feel again that spaghetti strap
Of a red negligee falling off my shoulder,
As I lie in bed between satin sheets.
(Maybe not satin, I might slip to the floor.)
Let me feel those cold oak planks beneath my feet.
I want to feel! I'm not dead yet, you know.

Come sit with me, even if the cat's got my tongue.
Just sit and read or do what you enjoy most.

Sharing oxygen in silence brings far more joy
Than a Q&A on what I had for breakfast
Or a game to jump start my memory.
Ah, memory. How I hate that word.

But listen. Since I don't plan to be old,
Come and let us just be.
Tell me a joke, take me to the mall,
Bring me a red rose, or simply sneak in
A glass of rosé. And laugh with me,
Dance with me, as we sip
Together in our Happy Hour.

DEAR WORLD

I defied death today.
Not by a pen like Emily Dickinson's
"Because I could not stop for Death –
He kindly stopped for me –"
Nor by Dylan Thomas's
"Rage rage against the dying
Of the light."

Oh no, Since money talks,
I did it that way.
A check to renew my membership to NCPA
Northern California Publishers/Authors
Not for a year but for TWO!
Hear that, and it's not refundable.
And I plan to collect.

Why Poetry

University of California, Berkeley, journalism student Holly McDede asked, "Tell me how your poetry has made a difference in readers. Can poetry really change us?" I told her my stories:

My first visit to Sacramento was to a church to speak on giving care to family members with Alzheimer's disease. The rather lengthy title of my talk was: *Bringing Compassion and Dignity to Our Alzheimer's Family through Poetry and Stories*. After my address, an elderly woman followed me and confessed, "You made me cry for the first time since I was fifteen years old. Your poems made me cry."

"Tell me your story," I said.

She rolled up her sleeve and showed me tattooed numbers on her arm. I needed no further explanation.

> I was fifteen years old when the guards came to take my father and two brothers off to Auschwitz. Mother and I knew we would be next. One day a doctor came to our house and gave us a letter he had written on his medical stationery. He said the letter would save us from the guards.
>
> He wrote that this woman has heart problems

and would be gone in a few days, and that I was also ill and would not survive any journey. My mother and I were so elated by the doctor's kindness, and we treasured his letter. We believed the letter would save us since it was written by a doctor on his stationery.

When the guards came knocking on our door one night, I proudly showed them the letter. They read it, laughed, tore it into shreds and took my mother and me to the train. When we arrived at Auschwitz, my mother was led to the left and I, to the right. The next morning, I cried and asked, "Where's my mother? I want my mother." A guard told me she was being cared for in a hospital. Each morning I cried and asked for my mother until one of the women told me, "See the smoke coming out of that stack? That's where your mother is." That day I promised myself I would never ever cry again. Nothing could be as bad as the day I lost my mother.

Today, your poems and story softened my heart, and I cried. It was frozen until today. Thank you.

I held her in my arms as we both wept, and I could only say, "Crying is good, isn't it?"

During my teaching career, poetry writing was always part of the curriculum. Stories about my students and their first experiences with poetry can be found in my book *Teacher, You Look Like a Horse.*

Since retiring, I've written five children's books based on a little mouse poet named Wordsworth. Wordsworth's ability to resolve human problems through poetry made a difference in readers' lives, as well as in mine. Here is a glimpse into each of the Wordsworth books:

Wordsworth the Poet: Being a poet makes Wordsworth different. Classmates made fun of him, and he caused worries for his parents, until his poetry helped them see that being different is special and worthy of respect.

Children who met Wordsworth at age six or seven are still sending me poetry as adults. Most importantly, many expressed new-found confidence in being different. At a school for autistic children, students wrote poems, like Wordsworth, that expressed how it felt to be treated differently. Once at a coffee shop, I became acquainted with a waitress whose sister was autistic. Her sister was introduced to Wordsworth at school, and the family thought it would be a treat to have her meet the author in person. We met at the coffee shop. The family was astonished when their daughter ran up to me, hugged me, and wouldn't let go. They stood there with tears in their eyes, saying, "She doesn't hug anyone." "She's not hugging me, she's hugging Wordsworth," I explained.

Wordsworth Dances the Waltz: Grandma is losing her memory, and Wordsworth reminds us through poetry that she is still Grandma, with or without her memory

A young mother confessed that her four-year-old daughter asked her, "Mommy, why do you talk so mean to Grandma?" The mother said her children have turned into Wordsworth and are helping her care for her elderly mother with compassion.

In a fifth-grade class, a student came up to me to say: "I wish my parents had this book; they are not nice to my grandma." I gave her a copy of *Wordsworth Dances the Waltz* to share with her parents.

One school made it a year-long project to visit a nursing home and record the residents' stories, after the students read *Wordsworth Dances the Waltz*.

Wordsworth! Stop the Bulldozer: Can Wordsworth and his friends stop the destruction of trees with their poetry?

This is an example of be careful of what you write. Young readers told their parents they should no longer have real trees for Christmas, they need to save trees by using artificial trees. I, too, have joined these families—how could I fill the house with the scent of fresh fir when my young readers are trying to preserve our forests?

Wordsworth! It's In Your Pocket!: Wordsworth's friends are addicted to electronic games and devices. Can he convince them to become his friends in person again?

I know one grandfather who collects cell phones at his front door and restaurant entrances, saying, "We're talking to each other." He is a rare exception, though. Since so many children and adults are already deeply addicted, this story may be too late to make a difference.

Wordsworth the Haiku Teacher: Wordsworth teaches readers how to write haiku poems.

Children and adults have not stopped writing haiku. They come to me through email and cards. Christine Reed, proprietor of Basically Books in Hilo, where we introduced *Wordsworth the Haiku Teacher* at a book signing, wrote a collection of haiku to help process her loss when her husband David died. She was surprised how haiku helped ease her grief. "I am still writing haiku in the middle of the night but am awake in the wee hours less often now."

> Night sounds all around
> In the depth of darkest hours
> Your presence is felt

Nancy Colden of Wisconsin, mother of a former third-grade student, sent this haiku with a note, "You would be surprised how many haiku I write. I see even a shoe, and it gets my mind going. We can find meaning in anything if we try."

> The poet teacher
> Gives life to Wordsworth the Poet
> Who teaches the World.

My niece Tammy Antonio began to communicate through haiku:

What a fun-filled day!
Food, fun, laughter, and a swim.
Wish it didn't end.

Soon after the Vietnam war, I met Darryl, who had completed his tour of duty and returned with a severe case of PTSD, so broken he was unable to be in a relationship. In Vietnam, he had been a helicopter pilot forced to play God, deciding which children should be left to die in villages that had just been bombed by our troops. I wrote this poem for him, which helped him slowly face his demons...not completely, but it was a start.

The Wooden Soldier

The wooden soldier marches
with his factory-made key.
Steadily, rhythmically,
mechanical precision.

The wooden soldier marches,
then comes to a halt,
a soldier no more,
just a wooden peg.

But the soldier I know
keeps on marching.
He never winds down,
can't turn himself off,
he has no key

to stop him from seeing
severed limbs of children,
scattered logs on battlefields.
Can't stop smelling
rivers of blood
on a Sunday afternoon.

Forgive us, O Soldier
For issuing keys
Only to soldiers
On wooden knees.

Forgive us, O Soldier
For mechanized birds,
Wooden logs and battlefields.

Almost twenty-four years later, this same war entered
my life through a third-grade student.

The signs were there: When students need to talk
they hang around my desk, playing with my stapler
or realigning my pens and pencils until there is
privacy for courage to emerge.

"Sometimes," she quietly started,
still playing with pencils,
"I get up at three in the morning
and hear my dad crying.
I go downstairs and he's sitting on steps,
crying in the dark.

He was in the Vietnam War; he won't talk about it
but I watch him cry a lot. He can't sleep.
I know because I always see him on the steps.
I wish I knew how to help him."

Damn! Here's that war again.
No child ought to be wakened at 3 a.m.
by a father's tears.
No child ought to be sucked in, to 25-year-old wars.
No child ought to have dreams
of brightly crayoned images
disrupted by black ashes.

I wasn't trained to undo the nature of war.
I didn't know how to banish the phantoms of war.
Maybe...maybe...I gave her a copy of *Golden Spike*.
"I wrote these poems about the war.
Maybe your dad will find this book helpful."

A few weeks later, she wrote in her class journal:
Private to Miss K:
My dad is always reading your book.
He carries it around with him and
he's not getting up anymore.
He's not crying anymore.
Thank you for helping him.
Is it okay if I keep the book a bit longer?
He wants to know,
did you know someone from the Vietnam War?
"Yes," I wrote in her journal.

"Tell your dad I knew someone just like him."

On the last day of school,
once again she stood near my desk.
"I'm sorry for not returning your book,
but my dad is still reading it.
I hate to take the book away from him."

"I gave that book to both of you.
I'm so glad my poems help him."
She held on to our hug, whispering,
"Thank you, Miss Kakugawa."

Holly sat and listened with tears in her eyes. I believe her question was answered.

Author's Note: Darryl's complete story appears in *Echoes of Kapoho* (Honolulu: Watermark Publishing, 2019).

FRANCES THE FRAUd III

Sometimes Wordsworth, my literary mouse poet, accompanies me on my walks. He tsk-tsks a lot when he sees how respectful friends are toward the Mall Poet. Leave it to him, he once again dug up another Frances the Fraud exposé. Be careful what and who you create. Here's Wordsworth:

Ah, I've done more detective work since her last book. The word "handcuffs" came to mind as I watched handcuffed immigrants being expelled from our country. It's a good thing the mall security guards aren't taking Frances away in handcuffs. Let me explain.

Frances, as you know, worked as a teacher for three years before she was asked to test a statewide language arts program for the island of Hawai'i. She was then invited to the University of Hawai'i to help develop a statewide literature program for the public schools. Next came several Department of Education positions at the state and district offices, interspersed with classroom teaching and lecturing for the College of Education, etc. Not bad for a teacher whose bachelor's degree was in preschool-primary education. Lucky for her, she had published a few books of poetry early in her career, and her publications were accepted in place of a graduate degree.

Yes. As always, Frances succeeded in maneuvering around her lack of skills and experience to reach her goals, for example by writing poetry for her music theory professor to get a passing A. She has avoided math her entire life. Her checking registers show account balances to the penny, but only because, if you look closely, there are plus or minus amounts added or deducted to match exactly with her monthly statements. At a school where teachers had to hand in the end-of-year attendance sheets, the secretary shook her head and even offered to take her out to lunch if her total came out right. This luncheon never happened during her years at the school.

So how did she pass those math courses to receive her teacher's degree? Easily, if you're Frances on the Kapoho Survival Plan. She chose to earn her degree in preschool-primary education to avoid all advanced math courses. She was determined not to fail and didn't, and she became a kindergarten teacher for the first few years of her career.

Wait, how was Frances accepted at the university when she was required to have two years of algebra and one of chemistry? She crocheted in chemistry class in the back of the room and received an A, because the teacher himself was not a qualified teacher. She passed her first year of algebra, but her school didn't offer Algebra II. The algebra teacher, who was also the athletic coach and who must have felt as inadequate as his students, invited her to sit in his Algebra I class. He gave her an Algebra II book to study, but not tests; and voila, she had both classes on record for her entrance to the University of Hawai'i.

One summer the University of Hawai'i offered Frances a six-week fellowship to study special education under one of the most renowned special education professors in the nation. She accepted the fellowship on condition that she teach special education for two years minimum. Her records show nada, nil, nothing of the sort although she did apply what she had learned from the fellowship in her regular classrooms. And she kept her special needs students in her class instead of sending them to special education classes.

The fellowship was a summer of inspirations. One day the professor appeared to be on edge. He explained, "Tonight I'm having dinner with First Lady Jackie Kennedy and Henry J. Kaiser, and I'm nervous as hell." Kaiser, the industrialist, had already built a school (named after him) and invested in real estate developments and other businesses in the islands.

The following morning, before the professor could begin his lecture, Frances raised her hand and asked, "How was Jackie Kennedy last night?" "I'm in love," the professor said. "She knew more about special needs children and adults than anyone I have ever met. She knew the details of current research being done in special education and shared how Joseph Kennedy, who had had a stroke, was benefitting from therapies based on research. Henry Kaiser, on the other hand, was a total jerk. Since he didn't go beyond high school and dislikes college grads, he completely ignored me. He especially looks down on professors, which was obvious as he never made eye contact with me. Ah, but Jackie, she was the most gracious woman ever."

Frances received an A for the six-week fellowship. I think it's because she attached a note to one of her papers, commenting on the professor's resemblance to a handsome television star. She watched him blush as he read the note.

There must have been something special in the Kapoho water tank, in addition to the mosquito wigglers that would often be found in glasses of water. There was always someone looking out for Frances. Or, more likely, she knew how to finagle others into looking out for her.

Oh, before I run off to the beach: If you should invite her to lunch, please don't serve her baloney or tuna sandwiches. I'll tell you about it in the next story; I'm not done yet.

Author's Note: Frances the Fraud I and II appear in *Can I Have Your Pearl Bracelet?*

It Can't Be All Bad

T his is Wordsworth again, my pen ready to answer the question journalist Holly McDede asked during her last interview with Frances: How did you become the kind of person you are today?

Frances would say that a culturally deprived environment, a poor-quality education and living in downstairs servitude made her who she is. I can say it better.

We all know she was delivered by a midwife in the most remote plantation village in Kapoho, now under lava. Until she was eighteen, the village had no electricity or indoor plumbing, which means she sort of grew up in the outhouse. Her teachers from grades one to six were high school grads because college-educated teachers wouldn't come to remote Kapoho. The teachers hadn't been trained and didn't know what to do, so they read to their students a lot, did gardening and taught them music from the only music book in the school: Stephen Foster's green music book.

It's a mystery how many of the books available to teachers were about slavery. Images of the auction blocks as families were being sold and separated sank into Frances' heart and stayed. They sang songs like

"Massa's in de Cold Ground" and other spirituals from the South.

It was Frances's dream to become a writer, and we both believe it was this lack of books and educational materials that helped her become the writer she hoped to be. The books and songs on slavery humanized her, and of course at age five, the bombing of Pearl Harbor and its aftermath had a profound impact on a child's emotions and her sense of self. In high school she wrote poems of the Korean War—all lost during the volcanic evacuation—but in later years, she managed to publish a book of poetry on the Vietnam War.

Another strong influence at age eighteen was the enormous transition from kerosene lamps to electricity, from outhouse to indoor plumbing, and from sharing futons on the floor with siblings to having her own room and bed. This was like suddenly time-warping a sixteenth-century young girl into the twenty-first century, and it happened when she started in Hilo. To earn her way, she worked as a live-in maid with a wealthy family while she attended the University of Hawai'i at what is now the Hilo Campus.

There were indignities she had to swallow, and each night she told herself, "Imagine you are in prison so you can become a teacher." The most difficult was eating in the kitchen while the family ate in the dining room. Back home, there were seven Kakugawas eating and chatting away around a long wooden table.

And yet, and yet, there were efforts made to help her feel more humane, more like a part of the family. Mrs. Evans, the woman of the house, made it clear that the word *maid* was not to be used. The children were not to know she was being paid $25 a month. Every day, a child was designated Child of the Day, and had the privilege of eating with Frances in the kitchen and sitting next to her in the car when they dropped her off at the college. But she was still the maid.

Frances seems to have a special angel who turns many negative situations into positive, humanizing experiences.

At the university, the Korean War veterans saw Frances's humiliation each morning when her *haole* employers, in their fancy vehicle, dropped her off for classes. These vets knew a way to help her feel less embarrassed: When she went to the snack bar to purchase a sandwich, it was paid for. She knew who her anonymous benefactors were after begging the cashier for names. Even at age eighteen, she knew how to preserve the dignities of donor and receiver; she kept the names to herself, never revealing them.

Psst...she did fail one course: Speech 100. Her pidgin dialect caused the Speech Board to fail her. But instead of ending her plans toward a teaching degree, one professor on the board suggested she attend a speech clinic for a semester. This clinic helped to improve her standard English speech, but leave it to Frances, there was another hurdle. "Good grief!" one professor on the board shouted, "Where did she get that Southern accent?" Her speech therapist was from the South! She passed the board and eventually earned her bachelor's degree in three and a half years. Ahem...she still has that pidgin dialect, though you can hardly tell by reading her written words.

The Hilo campus was a two-year college so she transferred to the University of Hawai'i at Mānoa campus. It still took great effort for Frances to survive. Once again, an angel in disguise appeared: A professor who had seen her work with his two daughters as a student teacher asked her to babysit once a week. They picked her up every Saturday, and more often than not, gave her a flimsy excuse that their plans had changed. Then they invited her to have dessert with the girls, paid her for a night's babysitting and drove her back to the dorm with another plate of dessert.

This was better than babysitting for families in faculty housing, standing uncomfortably as the professor dug in his pockets for change to pay her.

We can't forget her brother Paul, two years younger, who was paying for college by working at the Waikīkī Aquarium, sleeping on a cot behind the shark tanks. Frances loved running into Paul on campus because their conversations were a perfect script for her.

Paul: Do you have money?

Frances: Not really.

And Paul would hand her a few dollars

Now she could go to the snack bar, and instead of having those fifteen-cent baloney sandwiches that were her daily cuisine, she could splurge on the thirty-cent tuna sandwich that came with potato chips and a few pickle slices. This is why I put that little bug in your ear to keep baloney and tuna sandwiches off the menu; they still leave a bad taste in her mouth. Oh, and never serve her Libby's canned stew. Her Big Island classmates got to return home for spring break, but it was a hardship on Frances's parents, so she stayed in the dorm. Since the cafeteria was closed, she ate cold stew from Libby's cans. It was a lonely time for her.

In her youth, she did dream of living in New York, Paris and Hollywood, but she came to know that a carefree, entitled life would not have forged the character she needed to become a compassionate human being and writer of stories. And though I admit Frances did work harder than many of her friends, there was always someone who came to her aid with unexpected acts of kindness. And this, I think, made that difference in her life.

OK, I think I've answered Holly's question. I'm going to the beach...I have a poem to write...

– Wordsworth the Poet

LAST WORD

Be careful how you title your books. My wall, shelves and storage boxes display the beautiful gifts I've received, all directly related to my published book titles. After publishing *The Path of Butterflies,* for example, readers sent me gifts with a butterfly motif: butterfly tree ornaments, butterfly earrings, butterfly brooches and a real butterfly pinned and framed, which eventually turned into dust. I have a collection of Wordsworth the Poet ornaments to decorate an entire Christmas tree. And after my most recent book, *Can I Have Your Pearl Bracelet?*...yes, pearl ornaments, pearl bracelets and strings of pearls.

I am deeply curious and a bit wary about the title of this book. What will it bring? A few years ago, a reader from New York read my two Kapoho books where the outhouse was first introduced. She sent me—no, not a real outhouse, but a unique framed needlepoint artwork of an outhouse. She found the needlepoint outhouse at an art fair and bought it, not knowing why. She only knew she had to get it. It was never displayed on her wall; she just kept it in her basement all these years. After reading *Echoes of Kapoho*, she sent it to me with this note: "I now know why I bought this, it was meant for you."

So it looks like the outhouse has been taken care of. And please, I do not want to see a large semi-truck drive into our driveway with a real outhouse. I had thought seriously of naming this book *Can I Have Your Diamond Necklace?* but that would have been a bit too obvious, even for me!

My metaphorical mall outhouse, aside from the friendships and stories and poems it generated, produced yet another phenomenon that developed without any input from me. Words cannot fully describe the following. My in-residence poet/writer/editor Red Slider sensed from the very beginning that this mall outhouse is a one-seater, unlike the two or three-seater outhouses in Kapoho. Each morning he greets me on the front porch with, "So what's your mall story today?" He knows my mall friends by name, and yet he has never invited himself to join me on my mall walks. Some of my stories in this book have appeared in anthologies or in newspapers and no one has asked for the name of the mall, They, too, seem to know this is a one-seater mall. It is my hope that you are able to find your own special outhouse somewhere in a park, at a beach, or on the street where you live. There is a treasure waiting for you. Thank you.

– Frances

Morning Walk

Thank you, black crow
For your company this morn.
Are you Poe's raven
Calling Nevermore?

Thank you, majestic oak
For the symphony above
High C's, Low C's
A chorus of chirps, baton free.

Oh sparrows, sparrows
Wait, wait, you can't go.
Seven on a telephone line,
Complete your haiku ere you go.

Such was my walk this morn,
Outside the silent mall
With nature's best
For companionship.

The End

Afterword

Kevin Kawamoto, who wrote the Foreword to this book, sent an email regarding my choice of the word "outhouse" in the title of this book; he confirmed that the smelly connotation would not turn people off. I'd like to conclude by sharing with you his insightful comments about that word.

> This is the kind of book you'd want to take to the outhouse and savor one page at a time. Frances Kakugawa has taken an object—the outhouse—that is so often used as a symbol of poverty and cultural deprivation and given it a place of honor and affection, which it rightly deserves. Although rare today even in our rural communities due to improvements in infrastructure and public health practices, the iconic outhouse was a historical fixture in the lives of so many working-class families. Many of us have heard outhouse horror stories from our parents and grandparents, who want to impress on the younger generation how fortunate they are to grow up with indoor plumbing. The outhouse was rarely if ever discussed as an object of nostalgic charm, something that Frances comes close to doing.

But Frances uses the outhouse image to connect us to a bygone time and place where people worked hard, lived relatively rugged lives and stoically dispensed with the frills and luxuries of modern society that were far out of their reach. By claiming the family outhouse as a child's sanctuary from bothersome tasks and mundane chores and expanding it to a place of dreams and fantasies far beyond its immediate purpose, Frances embraces the outhouse image and turns shame into dignity, if not a kind of salvation. With her childlike memory, she wisely refuses to denigrate the outhouse and the community that surrounded it. Its presence was a necessity, plain and simple, and it served more than one purpose. Even today, nearly nine decades into the future, that outhouse lives on in the title of her nineteenth book. And Frances has transitioned during that time from out*house* to out*standing* poet and book author.

In this and her past works, Frances has not shied away from discussing her misfortunes and challenges; and that is good, because she has demonstrated that setbacks can be overcome and don't have to define one's future. It may take time, but the generation before her sacrificed so that she might one day be able to claim a more comfortable and enjoyable life than they did. Reaching for the stars is her way of showing them gratitude for what they endured. Surely they would be so proud to know that she can afford to buy the best toilet paper on the market today.

Thank you, dear Frances, for showing us how to be grateful for every day that we wake up in the morning and realize that we are able to enjoy, experience and explore the world around us for another day. May we each find our own "mall," befriend our own "mall rats," and look back fondly upon our own youthful "outhouse" that evokes warm memories of the sweet, lingering nectar of childhood safety and serenity.

Thank you, Kevin.

– Frances H. Kakugawa

Acknowledgments

This book took more than a village.

Editor Linda Donahue upped the ante on my writing. She edited out my Kapoho-style grammar, vocabulary, sentence structure and replaced my #1 Punctuation Rule: When in doubt, use a dash. Her honesty and language/writing skills are most appreciated with her deep friendship.

Kevin Kawamoto's foreword and afterword are examples of his encouragement all these years as someone who always saw more in my stories and poetry than I did. Once upon a time there was a little girl who always wanted to be a writer. But she lived in the outhouse and knew her pen would never be able to string words together to have a college professor say, "This is good." This is why she never took a poetry or writing course in college—she didn't want any professor to say, "You can't write." But lo and behold, today a professor told the little girl, now all grown up, "Your pen done good."

Charles Pellegrino has been here for me since the publications of my Kapoho books and his advice has become a mantra in my head. Reading his books also became lessons in writing. The best thing I did in 2010 was to challenge him in my blog over his book *Last Train from Hiroshima*. We were complete strangers then and he responded and here we are, friends across the continental US with his generous praise.

Dean Dorn. It was meant to be that we would become mall walker friends; I knew there was a reason I stopped him one day to chat. He saw more than I intended in my books when he discussed their stories and poems in relation to the sociological impact on life today. His contributions to this book are deeply appreciated.

Holly McDede was a student in journalism at UC Berkeley when she selected my work with poetry and caregiving for her graduate degree dissertation. It was an honor to spend time with her in interviews, on casual walks at the mall and in telephone conversations, and one of her questions became part of this collection. She is today a full-fledged journalist and her dissertation has gone public.

Leonard Chan of the Asian American Curriculum Project, who uses my work to promote peace and cultural understanding in communities, and Norma Jean Thornton of Northern California Publishers/ Authors for the title Poet Laureate of the organization. It is a privilege to share my poetry at their special events.

Photographer Tammy Antonio for creating magic in snapping a photo of me that doesn't scare children and household pets.

Dawn Sakamoto Paiva does magic with my manuscripts as seen in this book, cover to cover. She makes me feel I am her only client as her responses are immediate and her professional expertise, par excellence. Working with someone who has a Menehune in the house who makes her change her mind so often about her manuscript would drive anyone else insane.

Watermark Publishing: George Engebretson, for adding *The Outhouse Poet* to my list of books published by Watermark Publishing and for keeping the writer in me alive all these years. Knowing my work has a place to go to, and my pen is still not dry, inspires me to live with hope and optimism that this may not be my last book. It would take a lot of work to promote my books without Watermark staffers Kimi Patton and Julie Kaneko.

The walkers and workers at the mall who allowed me to use their names with their trust. "You can write anything you want about me," gave me the freedom to tell these stories. Included, too, are all the unnamed security guards, workers and other walkers who begin my days with affection, laughter and inspiration.

Finally, having two writers in the house may not be such a bad thing. Red Slider, writer/poet/editor-in-residence, understood the number of times I walked away from the middle of his sentence or conversation with, "I have an idea for a poem..." even when he had something significant to say. In these modern times, "I'm writing" replaces "I stay in the toilet," and he always hears me with his encouragement and input.

About the Author

Frances H. Kakugawa presently resides in Sacramento, California. Her books can be found on her website: www.francesk.org

Contact Frances online on her Facebook page at facebook.com/FrancesKakugawa or on her blog at franceskakugawa.wordpress.com

www.ingramcontent.com/pod-product-compliance
Lightning Source LLC
Chambersburg PA
CBHW051317120626
46547CB00015B/2273